WEST VIRGINIA'S
LONELY HEARTS KILLER

WEST VIRGINIA'S
LONELY HEARTS KILLER

The Vile Deeds of Harry F. Powers

ANGELA FIELDER

THE
History
PRESS

Published by The History Press
Charleston, SC
www.historypress.com

First published 2024

Manufactured in the United States

ISBN 9781467156165

Library of Congress Control Number: 2023946774

Notice: The information in this book is true and complete to the best of our knowledge. It is offered without guarantee on the part of the author or The History Press. The author and The History Press disclaim all liability in connection with the use of this book.

To the victims, may God's light shine upon you and His strength be your guide. Virginia, you are truly missed—may you find the peace and love on the other side that you were denied here on earth.

CONTENTS

FOREWORD

Welcome to the mind of the infamous lonely hearts killer of West Virginia, Harry F. Powers. This book sheds light on one of the most notorious serial killers in American history. Harry F. Powers, also known as the "West Virginia Bluebeard," gained notoriety for his heinous crimes in the 1930s. He preyed on vulnerable women through personal ads in newspapers, leading them to their deaths. In this book, author Angela Fielder delves into the twisted mind of Harry F. Powers and analyzes the social and cultural context that allowed his crimes to go unnoticed for so long. We also explore how modern-day society can still learn from this case, even though it took place almost a century ago.

But before diving into the details of Powers's killings, let us take a step back and understand why it is important to read about someone like him. As we go through the headlines today, we realize that not much has changed when it comes to crime. The term *Bluebeard* may have evolved, but women are still being targeted and victimized by men in positions of power. By understanding the story of Harry F. Powers, we can shed light on the dangerous patterns and behaviors that exist in our society and work toward preventing such tragedies from happening again. So, buckle up and join us on this journey as we uncover the chilling tale of the West Virginia Bluebeard. This is a story that needs to be told, for it highlights not only the dark side of human nature but also the resilience and strength of those who survived his reign of terror. As we delve into the details, let us remember to honor and respect the victims whose lives were brutally taken by this cold-blooded killer. Their stories should never be forgotten, for they serve as a reminder that we must always remain vigilant in the face of evil. And through the retelling of their stories, we can honor their memory and ensure that they will never be forgotten. So join us as we embark on this journey to unravel the mysteries of the West Virginia Bluebeard and learn from the lessons it has to offer.

Let us not turn a blind eye to the past but instead use it as a guide to shape a better future. So come along and read this book about the lonely hearts killer of West Virginia and discover the lessons that it holds for us all. Who knows, maybe by understanding the past we can prevent such tragedies from ever occurring again in our world. Let us take the time to learn and understand so that we may continue to move forward as a society, toward a safer and brighter future for all. So why should you read this book? Because it offers not only a true crime story but also lessons that can help us build a better world for ourselves and those around us. Let us not shy away from the darkness but instead use it as fuel to illuminate the path toward a better future. So, let's dive in and see what we can learn from the story of the West Virginia Bluebeard. Let us honor the victims and their families by acknowledging their pain and learning from it.

L.J. Nolen, DrPH
Researcher

PREFACE

When putting together the idea for this project, a myriad of things ran through my head. I would be remiss if I did not say that the idea was inspired in part by loss and grief. In seeking to understand why three special individuals were taken so heinously through murder, I decided to immerse myself in research on the psychopathic mind. I'd already been working on a continuation of research of sorts regarding the psychological innards of those who become contract killers and serial killers. It only made sense to take a "detour" into the predatorial mindset of men who murdered women and children for sport. Are they psychopaths? Are they sociopaths? Did their diabolical mindsets evolve, or were they simply born that way? What triggers them to turn on a proverbial kill switch when it comes to their targeted victims? And most importantly, why? Why kill at all?

These questions and more ran through my mind while conducting research on the lonely hearts killer of West Virginia (better known as the West Virginia Bluebeard), Harry F. Powers At the time of his crimes, the word *bluebeard* was defined as a man who killed women, namely women he may have had an amorous relationship with. While reading through the headlines, I noticed that many things have not really changed when it comes to crime. For one thing, there is always a motive. In Powers's case, it was money. In his mind, he felt entitled to the money that lonely widows had. It did not matter that he was a successful, married shopkeeper in Clarksburg, West Virginia. All that mattered to him was that he wanted more. He fancied himself to be the living, breathing American Dream that Horatio Alger once wrote about. His quixotic quest for wealth was a bit too ambitious to be taken seriously. After all, he was the son of a farmer who had immigrated to the American Midwest without any formal education or ties to the great American aristocracy. But that did not matter; in his mind, he was destined for riches and fortunes en masse, no matter who he had to kill to get it.

Speculation consumed me about the childhood of Powers. I wanted to know if he possessed the stereotypical profile of a serial killer. As I combed through the newspapers and court records at the West Virginia Archives, I did not find what I'd anticipated. All in all, Powers seemed to have a relatively normal childhood. Hiccups occurred during his adult years, when he stumbled into petty criminal activity that led him to serve time in prison. There were mentions in the court testimony of the scams and identities that he assumed as well as the insurmountable lies that he told. For Powers, lying was a lifestyle. But what led to the murders?

Mental illness is something that is rarely discussed when it comes to the West Virginia Bluebeard. Sure, the courts declared him mentally competent, but in 1931, there was no standardization across the country regarding the courts. Not to mention, the intersection of mental health and the law was blurred, if not ignored completely.

He didn't run. Actually, he never ran. Nor did he face his crimes as a man. Were it not for the lead detective on the case, Carl Southern, Powers would have undoubtedly continued to play the fool in court, always hoping to be declared legally insane. One of the key factors that worked in the favor of law enforcement is how they were relentless about contacting neighboring law enforcement officials and even writing to J. Edgar Hoover for clarification on the prison terms Powers had served in the past. Despite working fervidly to capture federal public enemies (such as John Dillinger, Baby Face Nelson, Bonnie and Clyde, Pretty Boy Floyd, Machine Gun Kelly and Ma Barker), Hoover also assisted law enforcement officials across the country in bringing murderers like Powers to justice. Those were the days when prisons were but a temporary stop along the route to the proverbial American guillotine, which in the 1930s meant death by hanging. Despite the endgame, Powers and others of his ilk preferred to live life on the edge, always thinking that they could outsmart law enforcement until the bitter end. And when the whirlwind of media swept into town, Powers took it all in, intrigued by the thought of headlines carrying his name, giving him the attention that his ego fervently sought. After all, some part of him desired attention.

When we think of the calculated manner in which Powers executed the murders of his victims, Russian novelist Fyodor Dostoevsky said it best in his book *Crime and Punishment*: "While nothing is easier than to denounce the evildoer, nothing is more difficult than to understand him." This sentiment rings true in all facets of studying the predatory mindset that serial killers like Powers possess. The whole notion of the haughty bluebeard lurking in the shadows is not new by any means. As a matter of fact, Powers was not the only bluebeard in twentieth-century history. The term originated from the French folktale of the same name. Written by Charles Perrault as one of the tales in his work titled *Histoires ou Contes du Temps Passe*, the story was first published in Paris, France, around 1697. The plot centers on a wealthy man who murders each woman that he marries and how his latest wife tries to avoid the same fate as the women before her. In its most popular iteration, the bluebeard marries six times and each woman he marries vanishes. As time progresses, his reputation precedes him and he sets his sight on the daughters of a neighboring nobleman. He marries the youngest daughter and gives her the keys to his castle with only one stipulation—she is not to open the door to an underground chamber or she will be punished. She agrees, and he goes off on a business trip. Overcome with curiosity, the woman opens up the secret chamber only to find the mangled corpses of the six former wives of the bluebeard. Upon his return, he discovers that she disobeyed him and decides to murder her. Cleverly, the young woman pleads with the bluebeard to allow her to pray with her sister (who had fled the castle seeking help). Just as the bluebeard is about to take her life, the woman's brothers arrive and kill him, resulting in his wife inheriting the castle and his fortune. The story ends with the widowed wife of the bluebeard cleaning up the murder chamber, providing proper burials for his wives and living happily ever after, remarrying another man.

Sadly, in the real world, the victims of men who are bluebeards rarely survive once they are ensnared in predatory traps. Additionally, contemporary bluebeards are con men; most are not wealthy and seek to take not only the fortunes away from the women that they marry but also any bit of dignity and self-preservation. These men prey on women, feeding steadily off of their vulnerabilities tied to romantic love. Such murderers unfortunately pad the headlines of newspapers, blogs and true crime shows daily. But what can be done to stop them? Awareness is the key to the prevention of further victimization. If people learn the signs to look for, then possibly they can aid their instincts and thwart the heinous predilections of the contemporary bloodthirsty bluebeard.

The tale of Harry F. Powers, the West Virginia Bluebeard, is dark, twisted and borders the macabre. Yet it also inspired three unforgettable literary works: two books, *Quiet Dell* and *Night of the Hunter*, as well as a movie, also titled *Night of the Hunter*. Within the pages of this book, readers will delve into the chilling world of a notorious serial killer who struck fear into the hearts of lonely women. He possessed the duality of being both a charming bachelor and a man with an insatiable hunger and thirst for violence who managed to leave a trail of devastation in his wake that still haunts parts of West Virginia today. By the end of his murderous reign, he became known as one of America's first serial killers.

Each page of this book takes readers on a bone-chilling journey that is sure to unravel the twisted psyche and heinous crimes committed by this infamous murderer. From his unsuspecting victims to his ultimate capture, this book is an unsettling quest to uncover what drove Harry F. Powers down such a dark path. This story is a glimpse into one of America's most haunting chapters—where lonely hearts found betrayal instead of love. The chilling tale of Harry F. Powers serves as a reminder of the dangers lurking behind seemingly innocent encounters. As readers delve into the depths of this book, they will uncover the sinister motives behind Powers's actions and the devastating consequences they had on his victims. This gripping account sheds light on the dark underbelly of romance gone wrong, leaving readers both captivated and disturbed by the true horrors that unfolded in West Virginia. However, it is important to note that the story of Harry F. Powers is just one extreme example of betrayal in the realm of romance. In reality, not all encounters result in such sinister motives or devastating consequences. It is essential to approach each relationship with caution and discernment, but it is also crucial not to let fear overshadow the potential for genuine love and connection. While the harrowing tale of Harry F. Powers serves as a stark reminder of the dangers lurking within romantic relationships, it should not discourage individuals from pursuing love and companionship. By maintaining a healthy skepticism and being mindful of red flags, one can navigate the treacherous waters of dating more effectively. Ultimately, life is about taking risks, and despite the occasional horror story, there is always the possibility of finding a genuine and fulfilling connection with another person.

ACKNOWLEDGEMENTS

Working on this book project would not have been possible without the help of numerous people. Special thanks to the Virginia State Archives Library and Museum in Richmond, Virginia. Also, many thanks to Ms. Debra Basham and the West Virginia State Archives in Charleston, West Virginia. Many thanks to Dr. Kendell Coker for the numerous talks (and coursework) on the criminal mind. I have to acknowledge retired special agent Daniel Reilly of the Federal Bureau of Investigation for clarifying forensic investigations and helping me better understand the criminal mind. Extreme gratitude is given to my son, Eli; my mother, Angela Beverly; Chantel; Tif; Chancie; and Kam. Thank you L.J. for your support. Thank you to Ms. Lynne and family. Kia and Ola, thanks for listening.

INTRODUCTION

Nestled deep within the rolling hills of Appalachia, Clarksburg, West Virginia, stands as a testament to the resilience of small-town America. With a recorded history dating to its founding in 1785, Clarksburg is a blend of heritage, traditions and timeless secrets. Once a pivotal stop on the road to western expansion and the bustling hub of the coal and glass industries, this town has seen more than its fair share of triumphs and tribulations.

At first glance, Clarksburg is a quiet American hamlet that exudes a bit of mystique. Its streets, lined with historic brick buildings and century-old homes, whisper tales of days gone by. Once upon a time before the Civil War, when West Virginia was not its own state, Clarksburg was a regional transportation center for the Baltimore and Ohio Railroad as well as the Northwestern Virginia Railroad. During the Civil War, the city was the quintessential trophy that both the Union and Confederacy were vying for. A former army quartermaster during the Civil War once described the city as "a motley collection of rickety frame houses, dirty looking brick dwellings and old stone buildings, some of which are propped up by large pieces of scantling, shattered monuments of the first families of Virginia."[1] Once it separated from the state of Virginia and became its own entity, West Virginia became a place where migrants flocked for opportunity. Italians from Calabria (in southern Italy) settled in Clarksburg to work in the coal mines. With them came a strong Roman Catholic community and the landmark Immaculate Conception Church. Along with coal production, natural gas led to a burgeoning glassmaking industry.

Boy in Tire Swing Holds a Cow by Its Halter, unknown, between 1925 and 1930. *Library of Congress*.

Architectural commissions were a mainstay in the community, and in the early part of the twentieth century, numerous architects were commissioned to design and erect the historic Goff Building on Main Street, the now defunct Waldo Hotel and the Union National Bank building, which still stands in the Clarksburg Historic District. By 1913, the Robinson Grand Theater had opened, and by the late 1920s, the theater had been electrically wired to feature films with sound. These were exciting times in the city, and it soon became known as a place where people knew one another, trusted one another and felt safe.

It was a quaint American town where neighbors were neighborly and looked out for one another. After all, nothing truly bad had happened since the Civil War and nothing truly bad happened at all. Appearances can often be deceiving. Beneath the veneer of Americana lay a tapestry of mysteries that have baffled, intrigued and haunted the residents for decades. Dark tales of unsolved crimes, family feuds and ghostly apparitions are as much a part of Clarksburg's lore as its pioneering past. Over the years, whispers and hidden truths have drifted through its valleys, making the town a magnet for those with a taste for intrigue.

Despite it being a place where life was peaceful and serene, it was also a town where your next-door neighbor could be a grocer, a banker, a coal miner or a heinous murderer. On August 28, 1931, the decaying bodies of two women and three children were found behind a garage belonging to a local Clarksburg grocer and his wife. At the time, nothing as horrendous as this had ever happened in the part of town known as Quiet Dell, let alone any other part of the state. And yet when murder came to town, it upended the lives of the very townspeople who desperately sought the solitude that the hills of West Virginia provided.

It is the story of the hunter and the hunted, the predator and the prey. In the grim tapestry of true crime history, few stories are as horrifying as that of Harry F. Powers, a cold-blooded serial killer with an insatiable bloodlust. His monstrous actions were driven not only by a desire for financial gain but also by an unnerving compulsion to extinguish the lives of vulnerable women and their children.

At its most basic, serial murder is defined by the Federal Bureau of Investigation as "the unlawful killing of two or more victims by the same offender(s), in separate events." The men and women in law enforcement who have dedicated their life's work to the capture and incarceration of serial murderers in the United States work tirelessly to learn the motives and mechanisms that drive serial killers to take the lives of innocent people so callously. Special agent Robert Ressler of the FBI's Behavioral Science Unit first coined the term *serial killer* in 1974 while facilitating a lecture at the Police Staff Academy in Bramshill, Hampshire, England, United Kingdom. Ressler was one of the founding members of the FBI's Behavioral Science

Unit, but prior to his work on serial homicide, select members of law enforcement worked independently to understand the criminal mind. In the late 1920s, when the FBI was in its infancy and under the direction of J. Edgar Hoover and his G-men, the process of capturing and executing the respective menaces to American society was in flux and well on its way to being reorganized. As a matter of fact, whenever law enforcement officials on the local level needed to verify information on a criminal, often they had to send official correspondence to J. Edgar Hoover, and he would send confirmation of a criminal's incarceration, noting the name of the prison that they were detained at and the length of detainment in his return correspondence. Thanks to technological advancement, procedures have changed since then, and law enforcement can perform these searches quickly.

The modus operandi of serial killers from the past and present still manages to perplex even the most astute law enforcement official. The reason being is that cases involving serial murder are complex, not merely due to the motive of the offender but more so due to the time span across the offender's murderous events. Serial killers methodically kill. That is, they plan their attacks meticulously. The kill is a game for them, and the police investigation becomes a tête-à-tête—a masochistic dance that the killer enjoys immensely. Further, the murders are rarely random—they are targeted. While such murders will inevitably involve many victims, the murder events can have a day, month or year timeline and can occur in several places. Podcasts and numerous shows on networks such as Investigation Discovery, Oxygen or even prime time television discuss serial killers ad nauseam. However, one key takeaway is that for every murder there is a victim, and each victim has a particular *victim profile*. On the surface, these profiles can seem a bit obscure. A basic victim profile could include being a woman and having certain vulnerabilities that would make an attack very easy. Understanding the profile of the victim helps law enforcement build a more in-depth typology of the serial killer.

In general, serial killers continue to captivate the public's morbid fascination with the criminal mind. This fascination inspires research to better understand the psychological factors driving the heinous, murderous acts of the serial killer. This story behind Harry F. Powers is an enigmatic look into the world and depths of the twisted mind of a lonely hearts serial killer while simultaneously exploring the dark motivations behind his gruesome acts of violence. To get a glimpse inside of the more insidious criminal mind can often satisfy the hunger for danger and the intrigue of personalities that are on the dark triad. It often provides an up close and personal account of the human predator and the murderous purview that they ascribe to. These tales from the dark side relate to the human condition, and they help people recognize the darker aspects of their own personalities while better understanding the "whys" behind the macabre act of murder. To get a bird's eye view of danger can be an expression of self-preservation that serves to mitigate the possibility of future victimization. However, in touring the minds of human predators, it is easy to forget that the story reopens the wound in the hearts of the families of the victims.

The Great Depression ushered in an era dominated by crippling poverty, criminal activity and a break in the traditional American familial structure. Americans were despondent and destitute, looking for a way out. Children worked in the fields and factories as adults labored wherever they could find work. The movie industry bustled with films that attempted to uplift the spirits of the weary by promoting an escape into a glamourous world where the good guys always won, the bad were always caught and true love was just over the horizon. The lure of romance was intoxicating, and for women who were young, the possibilities were endless, but for women who were a bit older and lost their husbands either through divorce or

Public health nursing made available through child welfare services. *Franklin D. Roosevelt Library Public Domain Photographs, 1882–1962, Collection FDR-PHOCO: Franklin D. Roosevelt Library.*

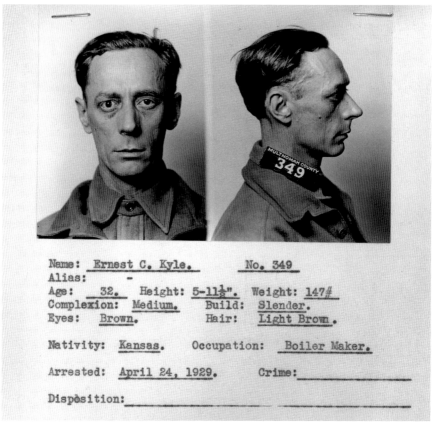

Mug shot with vital statistics, 1929. Investigation of Lester Case, et al., investigative case files, 1924–1933. *General Records of the Department of the Treasury.*

during the First World War, the possibilities were quite limited. So, many turned to placing lonely hearts ads that promised the right man access to a dedicated wife, her money and her undying love. Unfortunately, many lonely, well-to-do women whose ads were answered lost their lives on their quest for love.

The lonely hearts phenomenon was not native to the United States. In fact, women worldwide were placing lonely hearts ads in their local newspapers hoping to find love and protection in the arms of a stranger. Twelve years had passed since the end of World War I. And while people were experiencing a new normal, the war had taken a huge toll on women by negatively affecting their chances of getting married. The postwar period marked a time when women had minimal rights and were not taken seriously. In fact, most women were regarded as more than children but less than men.

Migrant worker on California highway, circa 1935. *Collection FDR-PHOCO: Franklin D. Roosevelt Library.*

Those who were not blessed with hefty dowries or inheritances had no other recourse but to rely on a potential husband for a sustainable future. Women, by and large, were raised to trust men blindly, but as the societal paradigm shifted, so did the mindset of a vast majority of women. Unfortunately, this

THE ONCE OVER
Lonely Hearts Column
By H. I. PHILLIPS
Copyright. 1928. by The Associated Newspapers

(With apologies to a tabloid newspaper feature.)

Lonely Hearts. I am a Swiss young lady, 24 years old, Presbyterian and fond of outdoor sports. Want to hear from a gentleman, well educated and with long eyelashes, who is fond of croquet. Must bring his own wickets and mallet.—Hilda.

* * *

Lonely Hearts. A rollicking outdoor girl with red hair and one gold tooth craves companionship of a tall man with a good tan who understands taxidermy, stamp collecting and other good clean fun. Am 38 years old and can recite Gunga Din. Wire or write.—Cynthia M.

* * *

Lonely Hearts. Something is all wrong with me. My doctor says it must be acidity or loneliness. Am not bad looking, know many two-syllable words, can blow smoke-rings and play xylophone if people insist. Would like to meet blonde woman between 26 and 40 with interest in roller skating and batik-dipping.—George.

* * *

Lonely Hearts. Businessman with comfortable home and blue shutters wants to form acquaintance of athletic young woman of unusual strength. Must be fond of strenuous exercise. I have automobile, player-piano and gout. Object: want some one to help put up and assemble parlor stove for winter.—Real Pal.

* * *

Lonely Hearts. Am a German girl, 29, blue eyes, black hair, Republican. Very fond of radio concerts, talking pictures, tomato bisque and sliding down banisters. People don't understand me. I long to know a nice, kind, middle-aged college man with a zither and no tariff views to speak of. One in a raccoon coat preferred.—Peggy.

* * *

Lonely Hearts. Good-looking young woman, 36 come next Candlemas Day, white, Irish, who loves to hitch-hike on fire engines in spare time, is anxious to meet a college boy with motorcycle and sea-sled. Would prefer one who doesn't toe in, sing Ramona and throw bottles when displeased.—Arabella.

* * *

Lonely Hearts. Widow with nine-story tenement on East Side would enjoy meeting a man who understands practical plumbing, wall-papering, ash removing and care of furnace. One who knows something about floor varnishing preferred. Good home, steady meals.—Mrs. X.

* * *

Lonely Hearts. Two sisters, Swedish, olive eyes, double chins, nice dispositions, would like to make acquaintance of a young society man who can make shadows, do card tricks, operate magic lantern and read loud from Police Gazette and Iron Age. Must look neat in straw hats and live in America.—Daisy and Moll.

* * *

Lonely Hearts. Home girl who finds most men uninteresting and who is anxious to know a man who doesn't follow the beaten paths and who will show her new phases of life. Must be some one of lofty ambitions, nerve, courage and determination with aptitude for outdoor life. Would consider flagpole sitter or human fly.—Gloria.

Opposite: Lonely hearts ads from the *Evening News*, Monday, November 5, 1928, page 14. *Newspapers.com*.

Above: Depositors in front of the closed American Union Bank in New York City, April 26, 1932. *Photographic File of the Paris Bureau of the* New York Times, *circa 1900–1950*.

paradigm shift did not occur until 1932. Had it occurred one year prior, perhaps a few lives would have been spared.

During the latter years of the 1920s, a predator arose in the United States that had never been seen before—that predator was known as the *bluebeard*. A bluebeard is a murderer whose moniker derives from the French fable of the same name. In the story, a wealthy nobleman murders all of his wives except for the last one, who manages to outsmart him and lead him to the same fate that he bestowed on each of his former wives. Coincidentally, one of the most notorious serial killers in France was none other than Henri Landru (the Bluebeard of Gambais), who murdered at least eleven women between the years 1915 and 1919 in Gambais, a province just outside of Versailles, France. Landru had a sick propensity for targeting, taking advantage of and murdering vulnerable, single women. He too relied on lonely hearts ads to find the perfect prey.

Right:
Woodcut *Barbe Bleue* (*Bluebeard*), published for the first time in *Les Contes de Perrault*. *Gallica Digital Library*.

Below: Henri Landru. *Wikimedia Commons*.

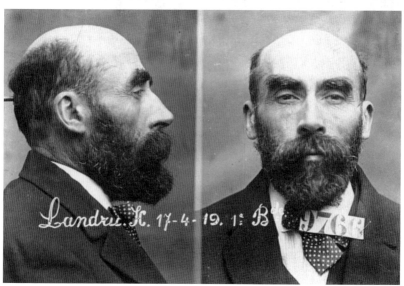

Much like his French predecessor, Powers stalked the lonely hearts ads nationwide in search of wealthy women to marry. Unlike Landru, Powers had but one motive—money. The women he killed were a means to an end. There was no deep-seated hatred of the fairer sex for Powers; he merely wanted to attain the American Dream and killed women and children to get

CL 574 Credit ACME 8-23-31. WV Archives Harry Powers' Case File - A18249.

close to it. For Powers, the women in the lonely hearts ads were dollar signs. His plan was simple: woo them, gain their trust, marry them and eradicate them. He even went so far as to build a murder garage where he would keep his "wives" prisoner, often starving them until they were too weak to fight. The clincher here is that Powers was already married to a woman who financed the shop that he owned in Clarksburg, West Virginia. He shared a home with his wife and her mother, neither of whom suspected him of being a serial murderer of women and children.

The thing about serial killers like Powers is that most are nothing like the knife-wielding madmen in contemporary horror movies. The most terrifying ones own homes and shops in cookie-cutter American towns that often have a charming Main Street chock-full of history. Harry F. Powers was just that type of monster. He blended into the tapestry of the sleepy hillside town that he lived in. Neighbors regarded him as quiet, and townspeople who frequented his store never expected him to be what he was—a most deadly conman who preyed on vulnerable, lonely women in search of true love. He played the role all too well, until the veneer of self-composure got in the way of what he desired—which was, of course, murder. A true killer for money, he lacked the modesty and sophistication that Landru had when drawing in his prey. He did, however, play the long con until the women no longer met his needs—then he disposed of them and their children.

Harry F. Powers preyed on the lovesick: the lovelorn, the lost and lonely-hearted women who had everything except for love. His downfall lay in the strand of arrogance that he had—he thought he would never get caught. It was inevitably the veneer of self-composure that stood in the way of his plans for murder, and once the veil was lifted, he could not stop the urge to eradicate his victims, stowing what he could not burn from their bodies in a subterranean section of his garage. In understanding the motive and possible hair triggers of Powers, it is imperative to keep in mind that "behavior reflects personality."[2]

Today, the concept of the lonely heart is readily apparent, as an increasing number of people seek love online, frequently traversing perilous pathways that lead to homicide in the name of love. History rarely changes; rather, it is cyclical and repeats. Unfortunately, people continue to prey on the vulnerable to satisfy their sick fantasies.

1

THE WHISPERS OF THE MADMAN

"They found five bodies. That's all they're going to find there." He smiled when he said that word "there" but he refused to say anything more about that.
—*Genevieve Forbes Herrick, the* Chicago Daily Tribune,
Monday, August 31, 1931

It was the eerie, spine-chilling manner in which Powers smirked when speaking about the remains of the women and children he'd murdered at his home that was not only par for the course for a demented personality such as his but also ignited fear where there was once hope in the hearts and minds of Americans at the start of the Great Depression. While the country was in a state of utter shock, he sat in his cell taking joy—reverie even—at the thought of all the attention and notoriety he received. Attention is what he craved from the media and the public, whom he perceived to be beneath him intellectually. This was his game. A sick dance between him and law enforcement. A tête-à-tête between his shadow personality, Harry Powers, and his true identity, Harm (Herman) Drenth—both of whom were fiends and true menaces to American society.

There was blood in the air for nearly two years prior to his arrest. And yet no one noticed anything out of the ordinary. Members of the greater Clarksburg community in West Virginia had not viewed Powers as having distinctly suspicious behaviors. His own wife, Luella Strother Powers, certainly hadn't seen anything unusual regarding her husband's actions. He was, more or less, living a normal life from her perspective. It

Above: Chicago Daily Tribune, August 31, 1931. *Newspapers.com.*

Opposite, top: Speaking of Superfluous Starlings, January 10, 1930. *Records of the U.S. Senate, Record Group 46.*

Opposite, bottom: Harry Powers. *West Virginia Archives.*

made local citizens wonder how it was possible a woman of Luella Powers's status could not have known something—anything—about her husband's murderous proclivities. As time would reveal, law enforcement officials weren't entirely convinced that the missus wasn't an active participant in the murders. They knew, even back then, that water seeks its own level in relationships, and thus Luella was somehow connected to the crimes. After all, she was all too eager to share her wealth with Powers, and rumor had it that once upon a time, her first husband was in the murder business as well.

WHO WAS HARRY F. POWERS?

Harry F. Powers was born Harm Drenth in Beerta, Netherlands, in 1893. The third of four children, Drenth was the son of a farmer, Wilko Drenth, and his wife, Jantje Drenth. While work on the farm provided a modest living for the family, it just was not enough. From a young age, Powers witnessed the daily struggles and hardships his parents faced living in rural isolation. As times grew tougher in the Netherlands, his father decided to relocate the family to Iowa, where other Dutch farmers were prospering.

In 1909, when Powers was still a teenager, the family finally arrived; however, after settling in the Midwest, they still faced financial challenges. This experience may have had an indelible effect on Powers, influencing his feelings of resentment and fostering a desire for control and dominance over his income and life in general. These early seeds of anger would later manifest in his violent actions toward women.

It did not take long for Powers to know that farm life was not for him. He wanted to live a life of leisure—but not on his own dime. As a result, his criminal tendencies began to surface. By the time he was seventeen years old, he'd resorted to thievery, stealing cars and liquor. On the outside, he appeared to be quite ordinary, yet there was something devious about him. Fraudulent schemes, deceit and manipulation became recurrent themes in his life, further solidifying the darker aspects of his personality.

No stranger to law enforcement, Powers was the type of person who welcomed trouble with open arms. His petty crimes eventually led to incarceration. However, after his release from his prison stints, he continued his criminal activities. He scammed people out of their money by posing as a wealthy businessman and swindled them out of their savings. He found it quite easy to steal money from women due to their nurturing and trusting nature.

As with anything else, success occurs when opportunity meets preparation. This adage rings true with criminal activities as well. Powers knew this all too well, and he took the time to ensure that he looked the part when it came to seducing his prey. In the sinister criminal underworld, even the most seemingly insignificant details can offer insights into the mind of a criminal. Such is the case with Powers, whose deceptive attire played a role in concealing the dark truth behind his charming façade. Even something as insignificant as his choice of clothing played a crucial part of his cunning modus operandi. In order to present himself as a respectable and successful businessman, he carefully selected his clothing to exude an air of prosperity and sophistication. Powers accomplished this by wearing suits and formal attire, complete with ties, polished shoes and heavy, thick-rimmed tortoiseshell Windsor glasses. This polished appearance allowed him to gain the trust of his victims and those around him.

Powers's choice of clothing extended beyond mere appearances; it played a role in projecting an aura of confidence and authority. By dressing sharply and impeccably, he aimed to instill trust and respect in those he interacted with, leaving them unsuspecting of the darkness that lurked beneath the surface. One of the most chilling aspects of Powers's deceptive attire was its versatility. His ability to shift between various personas made it easier for him to adapt to different situations and lull his victims into a false sense of security.

As part of his modus operandi, Powers presented himself as a grieving widower seeking companionship. To appear more sympathetic and relatable, he would occasionally wear somber and mournful attire when corresponding with his victims. This portrayal of a man recovering from loss helped him manipulate the emotions of the vulnerable widows he targeted. When portraying himself as a loving and devoted partner, Powers would dress in more casual and approachable clothing. However, when he needed to assert control and dominance over his victims, he would switch back to his more formal and authoritative attire, reinforcing his role as a man of influence. The clothing choices also served to manipulate the perceptions of those around him. By donning upscale attire, he convinced others of his financial stability and social standing. This manipulation allowed him to gain access to women of means, who would have been less likely to fall for his ruse had he appeared destitute or disheveled. Powers expertly tailored his appearance to fit the roles he needed to play. However, beneath the polished surface lurked someone altogether more sinister—a bloodthirsty monster—demonstrating that true evil can lurk behind even the most impeccably dressed exteriors.

Powers's ability to manipulate his image extended beyond just his appearance. He skillfully crafted a charismatic persona, charming those around him with his wit and charm. Because of his apparent sincerity, this façade made it even more challenging for his victims to detect his deception. However, behind the mask of charm and sophistication, Powers reveled in inflicting pain and suffering, leaving a trail of devastation in his wake. Despite his deceitful nature and lack of a moral code, Powers was able to marry well. He married a well-to-do woman who was no stranger to scandal.

THE MARRIAGE TO LUELLA B. STROTHER

The marriage between Harry F. Powers and Luella B. Strother shows that dark secrets can lay hidden beneath the surface of any relationship; however, sometimes women can knowingly form unhealthy attachments to men who are criminals. It is quite possible that Strother was a passive hybristophiliac—that is, a person who is attracted to and sexually aroused by people who have committed cruel and heinous crimes such as rape and murder. Consider the countless women who showed up to court to support Ted Bundy because they felt that he was "too charming" and did not look like the type of person who would rape, murder and dismember the victims. Strother was akin to those women. The passive aspect of the hybristophilia comes into play when a woman makes excuses for the behaviors and crimes of the criminal but has no interest in being involved with committing the crimes. Additionally, they tend to feel that the criminal in question would never—could never—hurt them in the manner that they were alleged to have hurt the victims. The disorder is considered a paraphilia, and it is also known as the Bonnie and Clyde Syndrome. Women tend to acquire the disorder more than men, and with Powers being adept at manipulation, it probably exacerbated the disorder in Strother. Further, in many ways, the danger of it all was a most tantalizing aphrodisiac to her.

In the forthcoming chapters, it will be revealed how Strother and her sister may have covered up for the more heinous murders committed by Powers. While it is easy to feel sorry for Strother, many people in Clarksburg at the time thought that she may have played a role in the murders. There was speculation that Strother had a penchant for low-caliber men. While she was cleared of having anything to do with the murders, information came to light that her first husband was actually a menace to society as well. His name was Ernest Keniseley, and he was tried for murder in 1903 when he killed a man with a rock. As luck would have it, Keniseley was acquitted of the crime due to pleading self-defense. Strother quickly divorced him and a few years later married Powers. The interesting thing here is that Strother was no stranger to answering lonely hearts ads, as that is how she met her first husband.

To understand Strother, and why she would marry a man like Powers, a bit of background is needed. In the 1920s, West Virginia was quite different than it is today. The state thrived after the Civil War until 1921 due to the expansion of the railroad. The coal mining towns in other parts of the state were bustling with workers from diverse nationalities; however, work conditions were perilous, and workers, union organizers and coal mine owners were at odds and continually feuding. Clarksburg, on the other hand, was thriving and had a solid residential middle class.

Wife of slayer. *West Virginia Archives*.

Clarksburg's prosperity was largely attributed to its thriving manufacturing industry, which attracted skilled workers and contributed to the growth of the middle class. The city boasted numerous factories and industries, such as glass manufacturing and furniture production, providing stable employment opportunities for its residents. This economic stability in Clarksburg contrasted sharply with the volatile and often dangerous working conditions in the coal mining towns of West Virginia during that period.

Luella B. Strother was a rather well-to-do woman who lived in Quiet Dell, West Virginia, a small town that lay five miles southeast of Clarksburg. Quiet Dell was a peaceful town, a middle-class enclave where time stood still and tranquility wafted in the wind. A financially independent woman, Strother owned a small store and a farm at a time when many people in the country were on the brink of financial disaster. The only problem (by society's standards) was that she was a divorcée, and while divorce did happen during that time, American society was traditional regarding marriage and rigid regarding women's rights.

Strother had bought lonely hearts ads from the American Friendship Society in the past, and this time was no different. She placed an ad in the *Lonely Hearts Magazine*, and it was quickly answered by Powers, who presented himself as a successful businessman. However, he was on the prowl for a new target—a wife—and Strother was none the wiser. She introduced herself as "Lulu" and told him that she lived with her sister and mother. When she told him about her store and land, he was all in. In her letters to Powers, Strother mentioned that she was forty-two years old and often referred to him as *dearie, honey man, dolly dimple, sugar lump, cutie* and *darling man*. Strother made it a point in one of her letters dated June 26, 1926, while he was residing in Crestline, Ohio, to mention that she preferred using the *Lonely Hearts Magazine* to find her "true lover." Further, she claimed that she did like the male offerings in the greater Clarksburg area.

The two married in June 1927, and they settled down in Strother's home at 111 Quincy Street in Clarksburg, West Virginia. Within three months, Strother's mother had died, and Powers managed to secure a job as a vacuum salesman. However, Luella's sister, Eva Bell Strother, was still alive and co-owner of the store, the house and the land that accompanied it. Powers managed to convince the two sisters to sign power of attorney to him, and his wife did not hesitate to do so.

Just prior to marrying Strother, Powers resided in Mansfield, Ohio, and attempted to swindle a woman there by the name of Lena Fellows, whom she met through a lonely hearts ad that he placed in Hammond,

Powers and Luella. *West Virginia Archives, Harry Powers' Case File.*

Indiana. Lena quickly fell for his schtick, and when he proposed, she eagerly accepted. Powers convinced Fellows to elope with him and bring all of her money and jewelry with her because they were not going to return to Indiana. Fellows did not question him and honored his request. When he arrived to pick her up at her house in Indiana, she immediately noticed that he looked nothing like he described himself in his letters. But she was so charmed by his mannerisms that she threw caution to the wind and left with him. A major reason why she left with him so abruptly is that she was eager to be married. It is unclear if her first husband passed away or if he divorced her. Nonetheless, she wanted to be married, and nothing would stop her from attaining that goal. When she hopped in the car with Powers, she was unsure of where they were going until Powers stopped at a nearby gas station. While there, Powers suggested that she lock her jewels and money in her suitcase prior to going to the ladies' room. She agreed and did so prior to using the restroom. Upon her return, she found her new husband had disappeared with all of her money and jewelry.

Powers did not get far before being captured and tried for the theft. To Fellows's chagrin, Powers was found not guilty of the theft, and then he quickly moved on to Strother. Ironically, Powers decided against murdering both Fellows and Strother. It is not known why; however, it can be speculated that Powers enjoyed the financial stability that Strother afforded him and possibly the fact that as long as he was married to her, she could look the other way when it came to his flaws and, most importantly, his crimes.

By all appearances, Powers presented himself to be a dedicated husband and a hardworking, productive member of society. His wife trusted him and supported him unconditionally, even when he was suspected of the murder of a former business acquaintance—Stamates Sfikas, whose body was found in the woods not long after the Eicher family. However, as the investigation unfolded, it became clear that Powers had been leading a double life. He had meticulously planned and executed the murders of both Sfikas and the Eicher family, revealing a sinister side that his wife had never known existed. This revelation shattered her trust and forced her to confront the harsh reality that she had been living with a man capable of such heinous acts.

WOMEN WHO MARRY SERIAL KILLERS

To understand the perplexing, captivated and eerie phenomenon of women entering into marital relationships with convicted serial killers, it is necessary to review the insatiable urges that drive them into the arms of these killers. Luella Strother was one such woman who possessed this widespread curiosity and macabre fascination. It seems hard to believe that Strother was completely in the dark when it came to her husband. After all, *how could she not know?*

One significant motivation observed in women who marry serial killers is their desire for fame and notoriety. These women are attracted to the attention and media coverage that comes with being associated with a notorious criminal. The media often sensationalizes these relationships, creating a cult-like fascination around both the killers and their partners. The women may seek validation and derive a sense of importance from their association with someone who is considered evil and dangerous.[3] Psychopathological elements play a significant role in the personalities of the women who marry serial killers. These women often exhibit shared psychopathy traits that make them particularly drawn to individuals with criminal tendencies. The allure of danger and deviance appeals to their own hidden desires and morbid fantasies. Additionally, they tend to exhibit codependent tendencies and attachment issues, seeking validation and affection from individuals who possess dominant and powerful personalities.[4]

Another possible motivation observed in women who marry serial killers is their quest for power and control. These women are attracted to the psychological dominance and manipulation exhibited by the killers. By associating themselves intimately with these individuals, they can exert control over them and manipulate them to fulfill their own psychological needs. Additionally, the women may identify with the power the killers possess and seek to replicate that power in their own lives.[5] In the case of Luella Strother, there is no record of her publicly exhibiting the need for power and control; however, the letters that she wrote to Powers indicate codependency, serious attachment issues and a penchant for manipulation.

One striking element about women who marry serial killers is the significant proportion of them who have a background marked by childhood trauma. Painful early experiences such as frequent abuse, neglect and abandonment in their family dynamics often form the foundation of their future relationships. Broken families, dysfunctional environments and experiences of abuse shape their perceptions and interactions in later life. Chronic feelings of neglect and abandonment during their formative years can lead these women to seek solace in manipulative and dominant individuals, such as serial killers. Another common characteristic among these women is the presence of personality disorders. Traits of Borderline Personality Disorder, Narcissistic Personality Disorder and Antisocial Personality Disorder are often observed in them.

Impulsivity, instability in relationships and chronic feelings of emptiness are indicative of Borderline Personality Disorder. Additionally, grandiosity, a craving for attention and lack of empathy are observable traits in these women, similar to Narcissistic Personality Disorder. Furthermore, they also show traits parallel to Antisocial Personality Disorder, such as disregard for and violation of the rights of others. The psychological profiles of these women are also influenced by their past relationships and experiences. Patterns of abusive relationships and unresolved emotional traumas are common occurrences in their past, potentially normalizing violence and manipulation to the point where they not only accept but also seek such relationship dynamics.

Interestingly, these psychological profiles seem to form a bridge connecting these women's motivations and the dynamics of their relationships with serial killers. The intricate relationship dynamics within marriages to serial killers are further examined in the ensuing section. Marriages to serial killers are characterized by significant power imbalances and control exerted by the killers over their partners. These power imbalances and control are perpetuated through various psychological manipulation techniques employed by the killers in order to establish dominance and control.[6] Serial killers often use fear and intimidation tactics to silence and manipulate their partners, creating an environment of subservience and obedience.[7]

These types of unions commonly feature emotional attachment and idealization. Within these relationships, a psychological phenomenon known as Stockholm Syndrome can be observed, where victims develop empathy, affection and even love for their captors.[8] Emotional attachment is further reinforced by cognitive dissonance and rationalization, as partners may downplay or justify the horrific acts committed by the killers, thus maintaining the illusion of a normal relationship.[9] Intimate relationships with serial killers often stem from psychological motivations centered on seeking emotional and sexual gratification. Some partners are attracted to the thrill and excitement that comes with being involved with a dangerous individual.[10] Furthermore, these relationships can fulfill specific fantasies and eroticization of violence for certain individuals.[11] The emotional and sexual gratification derived from these relationships arises from a complex interplay of psychological factors and societal influences.

The media plays and has played a crucial role in shaping public narratives and influencing individuals' perceptions of crime. The constant coverage and sensationalism of serial killers in the media contribute to a cultural fascination with crime, ultimately influencing women's decisions to marry serial killers.[12] During the time that Powers committed his crimes, the weekly newspapers were flooded with headlines of crimes being committed coast-to-coast and the FBI's most wanted list. It is possible that the coverage of other criminals led to the romanticization of Powers.

In contemporary society, due to the shocking nature of their crimes, serial killers often become subjects of sensationalism and romanticization. Media depictions portray them as mysterious and charismatic, thus appealing to individuals who may be seeking forbidden and dangerous relationships.[13] Women who marry serial killers may be drawn to the allure of forbidden and dangerous relationships. These relationships hold a particular psychological effect due to their societal "taboo" elements, making them appear more thrilling and enticing.[14] In addition, social isolation and marginalization can contribute to the vulnerability of these women, leading them to seek connection and power in relationships that are deemed inappropriate by society. When it comes to the decision to marry serial killers, there are several societal factors that play a significant role. These factors are deeply intertwined with media influence and cultural fascination with crime, which can distort perceptions and romanticize the actions of these criminals.

The media wields immense power in shaping society's perceptions and piquing its interests. In particular, the public's fascination with crime, especially sensationalized and high-profile cases involving serial killers, has created a strong demand for related content. This demand has given rise to a plethora of documentaries, books, movies and TV shows that cater to the curiosity of the masses. The media, in turn, obliges by providing extensive coverage, generating high viewership and readership. Consequently, women who choose to marry serial killers may find themselves exposed to glamorized and misleading portrayals of these criminals. As a consequence, they develop a distorted view of their personalities and a romantically idealized perception of their actions.

The media often indulges in sensationalism, which leads to the romanticization of serial killers. This unhealthy glorification can create an undeniable allure, particularly for vulnerable individuals. Serial killers are sometimes depicted as enigmatic figures who possess a certain charm, intelligence and allure that draw individuals toward them. The media's portrayal of these criminals as "bad boys" or "misunderstood geniuses" blurs the line between reality and fantasy, further fueling the dangerous fascination surrounding them.

Forbidden and dangerous relationships have always held a captivating allure that captures the imagination. The act of engaging in such relationships offers a sense of rebellion and escape from the mundane, particularly for individuals who feel marginalized or socially isolated. The societal taboo that surrounds these relationships adds an element of thrill and excitement, amplifying their appeal. Moreover, marrying a serial killer represents a power dynamic inversion. It challenges traditional gender roles, as the woman assumes a role traditionally associated with men. In doing so, she attains an unconventional form of power and control over her spouse, adding yet another layer of complexity to an already complex decision.

In today's society, there has been a growing interest in the phenomenon of women marrying serial killers. This analysis sets out to explore this complex topic from diverse perspectives, shedding light on the various motivations and implications involved. To begin with, our study has unearthed multiple motivations for these women, which encompasses a range of factors. Some seek fame and notoriety, while others are driven by deep-rooted psychopathological elements. Additionally, a desire for power and control has been identified as a key motivator. Delving into the psychological profiles of these women, it has become evident that they share certain psychopathy traits and personality disorders. Furthermore, their past relationships and experiences play a significant role in shaping their decision to marry serial killers. When examining the dynamics of these marriages, a pattern emerges. Power imbalances, emotional attachment, idealization and gratification are prominent features. These complex dynamics ultimately contribute to the longevity of these relationships. It is important to recognize that the consequences of women marrying serial killers extend beyond the individuals involved. They have profound implications for society as a whole.

The potential normalization of violence and the romanticization of crime and criminals pose significant challenges to prevailing societal narratives around crime, punishment and justice. In the case of Powers, him having access to a plethora of women across the country who were ready and willing to take steps toward not only meeting him but also moving in and marrying him was unnerving. This was a time when women were discerning when judging a mate. This was also a time when women were judged harshly for not being married. The following chapters reveal how many women would come forward to the authorities when Powers was in custody claiming to be engaged to him—one even claimed to be his wife—despite the horrors that this man committed. Understanding the mindsets of these woman can be helpful in finding the hidden truths in this case. What can be discerned here is that Luella may very well have been just as psychologically damaged as Powers, only she was better at hiding it. And while no charges were brought up against Luella or her sister, Eva, that does not mean that they did not play a huge role in the murders of the two women and three children. Luella seemed to live a rather quiet existence after Powers was executed, living on to age sixty-eight before passing away in 1957.

2

THE CON

One day men will look back and say I gave birth to the twentieth century.
—Jack the Ripper

I f there was one thing that Powers accomplished in life, it was that he was the living embodiment of the above Jack the Ripper quote. Certainly, he wasn't the first serial killer in America; there were a few who set the precedent for serial murder prior to Powers. Two of the more renowned serial killers that dominated headlines prior to Powers were none other than H.H. Holmes and Albert Fish. All three of these men were con artists—proficient at manipulating the vulnerable, lying pathologically and lulling unsuspecting victims to a most gruesome death. The only difference is that Powers received great arousal from the hunt, the lure, the murder and the final denouement or the swindling of his victims out of their finances. Interestingly enough, one of his alleged former lawyers, Evan Allen Bartlett, wrote a book on his criminal undertakings. The book, titled *The Love Murders of Harry F. Powers: Beware Such Bluebeards*, delves into the chilling details of Powers's crimes, shedding light on his twisted psyche and the methods he employed to deceive his victims. Bartlett's account offers a haunting glimpse into the mind of a man who thrived on both psychological manipulation and financial exploitation, leaving a trail of devastation in his wake.

BACKGROUND OF THE BLUEBEARD

The targeted killings committed by Powers were not unusual. His style of murder was likened to the fictional bluebeard of French literature. At a glance, the term *bluebeard* might be reminiscent of the fable by Muhsin Mahdi titled *1001 Nights*; however, the antagonist in this story (King Shahryar of Persia) does not precisely exemplify the characteristics of a bluebeard in a historical context. When confronted with the term, many people might think of pirates; however, the term dates back centuries to Europe.

The origins of the French Bluebeard character can be traced back to ancient myths and legends. Various cultures possess tales of husbands with murderous tendencies, often distinguished by unique physical features. These earlier renditions paved the way for the archetype that ultimately became Bluebeard, with his iconic blue beard serving as a distinct visual identifier. Furthermore, Bluebeard's presence in European folklore manifests in the existence of similar characters found across different cultures. For instance, tales of husbands concealing secret rooms or demonstrating ruthless behavior toward their wives can be discovered in various European nations, including Ireland and Sicily. These commonalities underscore the widespread nature of the bluebeard archetype and its enduring appeal within diverse literary traditions.

European folklore describes the bluebeard as a sinister being who marries and murders a series of wives. Charles Perrault's "Bluebeard" was first published in 1697 as part of his collection *Mother Goose Tales*. Perrault's rendition recounts the tale of a wealthy nobleman who takes a young woman as his wife. The nobleman, distinguished by his blue beard, entrusts the woman with a set of keys and instructs her to explore the castle during his absence. Despite his warning to never enter a specific room, the woman's curiosity overpowers her, leading to a chilling discovery of the lifeless bodies of Bluebeard's former wives. Perrault's depiction of Bluebeard had a profound effect on subsequent interpretations of the character. By emphasizing the theme of forbidden curiosity, Perrault tapped into a universal human emotion, shedding light on the dangers that arise from pushing beyond the boundaries set by those in power. Furthermore, Perrault's narrative introduces a moralistic aspect to the character, elevating Bluebeard from a mere villain to a cautionary figure who serves as a deterrent against curiosity and disobedience. This cautionary element has resonated deeply with audiences and influenced countless adaptations and reimaginings of the French Bluebeard character throughout the centuries.

The portrayal of the bluebeard in both the nineteenth and twentieth centuries differs a bit. In the nineteenth century, Honoré de Balzac's depiction of Bluebeard reveals a complex figure entangled in sociocultural constraints. Balzac does not simply present Bluebeard as a tyrannical despot but as a captive within the intricate web of societal norms and expectations. In contrast, Gustave Flaubert delves into the timeless aspects of the Bluebeard character. Flaubert emphasizes the psychological intrigue surrounding the character, blending reality and surrealism and highlighting the adaptability inherent in the Bluebeard narrative. In the twentieth century, feminist literature wielded the Bluebeard tale as a symbol of male violence and oppression. The character's implicit misogyny sparked critical debates on patriarchal norms, effectively situating the narrative within the context of feminist literary analysis. Surrealistic works of the era viewed Bluebeard as a product of psychological grotesquery, propelling the narrative into darker, dreamlike realms. Bluebeard's oppressive nature was deciphered through the lens of subconscious symbolism and irrationality, giving the character an entirely distinct, surrealistic dimension. This aspect of violence was prevalent in earlier ideations of the character. For example, Jacques Offenbach's opera *Barbe-bleue* (1866) takes the character and reimagines it within a theatrical setting, delving into themes of power, deception and secrecy, unraveling a stage presentation that showcases Bluebeard's dark masculinity, inherent violence and manipulation. With regards to Harry F. Powers, the bluebeard trope was indeed one of violence, mass manipulation and irrationality.

THE BLUEBEARD OF GAMBAIS

A decade prior to Powers's reign of murder, his French counterpart Henri D. Landru (known as the "Bluebeard of Gambais") committed a series of similar atrocities in Paris from 1915 to 1919. Landru was executed in 1922 via the guillotine, and his head was preserved and used as an artifact in the Hollywood, California location of the Museum of Death. It was alleged in *The Love Murders of Harry of Powers: Beware Such Bluebeards* that when Powers was detained for questioning, the police inquired if he had ever heard of Landru, to which he merely gave a blank look. Further, they asked if Powers had studied the crimes and murderous methods of Landru. Powers did not answer the question. The crimes of both Landru and Powers were quite similar, and there was a short window between the time that Landru was executed in 1922 and when Powers began his crimes in the 1920s. The police were intrigued by the striking resemblance between Landru's modus operandi and Powers's own criminal activities. They wondered if Powers had drawn inspiration from Landru's notorious case, which had garnered significant media attention at the time. However, Powers's silence left them with no concrete evidence to establish a direct connection between the two criminals.

THE LONELY HEARTS HUNTER

I could not help the fact that I was a murderer, no more than the poet can help the inspiration to sing.
—*H.H. Holmes*

Powers wasn't always the slick con artist who fleeced well-to-do women out of their money and their lives. It took time for him to progress to this level of crime. But once he realized how easy it was to get money on false pretenses, there was no stopping him. Powers's transformation into a skilled con artist was fueled by his realization of the lucrative opportunities that came with deceiving wealthy women. With each successful scheme, his confidence grew, and he became more adept at manipulating his victims. This gradual progression ultimately led him to commit heinous acts, leaving behind a trail of shattered lives and unanswered questions for law enforcement to unravel. Indeed, con men were common in the United States. During this time, the lack of proper regulations and oversight made it easier for con men like Powers to thrive. The allure of quick wealth and the constant influx of new potential victims ensured that the scam artist profession remained a persistent problem in society. The rise of industrialization and urbanization also contributed to the proliferation of con men during this era. As people flocked to cities in search of opportunities, they often found themselves vulnerable and easily swayed by the promises of these deceptive individuals. The lack of community ties and the anonymity of city life made it easier for con men to operate without detection, further fueling their illicit activities.

It just so happened that the owner of the Detroit-based American Friendship Society, Albert Plater (also known as Albert Broel), and his wife, Olga, had a secret to hide. They were not only the editors of the *Lonely Hearts Magazine*—where Powers and Strother both placed matrimonial ads—but also experienced con artists who succeeded in getting hundreds of people to buy matrimonial ads and subscribe to the magazine. The American Friendship Society was considered one of many lonely hearts clubs (also known as matrimonial bureaus) in the nation. Plater's organization ran ads that noted the following in publications such as the *Los Angeles Illustrated Daily News*: "The World's Greatest Letter Club has many rich folks who seek new friends." Moreover, Plater was no stranger to conning people through impersonation. In the early 1900s, Plater was found guilty of impersonating a Russian count and an army captain. These impersonations allowed him to gain the trust of wealthy individuals and exploit their connections for personal gain. Despite his deceitful past, Plater's society continued to attract members who were hopeful of finding companionship and social status through the club's network.

While Plater's organization never directly aided and abetted the murderous proclivities of Powers, after the retrieval of the widow Eicher and her children from Powers's murder garage, the organization was branded a public menace that deliberately defrauded its patrons. Moreover, it unethically posed as a nonprofit organization and collected in excess of $100,000 in fees, which equates to more than $1.6 million in current dollars, over its four years of operation.

Fleecing the lonely in the 1920s was a big business. Once Powers realized how profitable it was, he jumped on the opportunity. It was easier than robbery or petty theft, and all that he really required was the proper

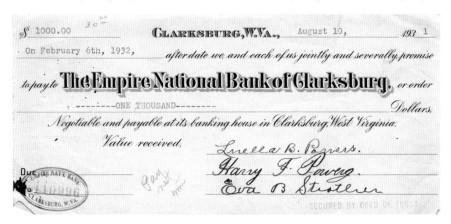

Above: Bank note for $1,000 signed by Harry Powers. *West Virginia Archives, Harry Powers' Case File.*

Opposite: Lonely hearts ads from the *Evening News*, Monday, November 5, 1928, page 14. *Newspapers.com.*

THE ONCE OVER
Lonely Hearts Column
By H. I. PHILLIPS
Copyright, 1928, by The Associated Newspapers

(With apologies to a tabloid newspaper feature.)

Lonely Hearts. I am a Swiss young lady, 24 years old, Presbyterian and fond of outdoor sports. Want to hear from a gentleman, well educated and with long eyelashes, who is fond of croquet. Must bring his own wickets and mallet.—Hilda.

* * *

Lonely Hearts. A rollicking outdoor girl with red hair and one gold tooth craves companionship of a tall man with a good tan who understands taxidermy, stamp collecting and other good clean fun. Am 38 years old and can recite Gunga Din. Wire or write.—Cynthia M.

* * *

Lonely Hearts. Something is all wrong with me. My doctor says it must be acidity or loneliness. Am not bad looking, know many two-syllable words, can blow smoke-rings and play xylophone if people insist. Would like to meet blonde woman between 26 and 40 with interest in roller skating and batik-dipping.—George.

* * *

Lonely Hearts. Businessman with comfortable home and blue shutters wants to form acquaintance of athletic young woman of unusual strength. Must be fond of strenuous exercise. I have automobile, player-piano and gout. Object: want some one to help put up and assemble parlor stove for winter.—Real Pal.

* * *

Lonely Hearts. Am a German girl, 29, blue eyes, black hair, Republican. Very fond of radio concerts, talking pictures, tomato bisque and sliding down banisters. People don't understand me. I long to know a nice, kind, middle-aged college man with a zither and no tariff views to speak of. One in a raccoon coat preferred.—Peggy.

* * *

Lonely Hearts. Good-looking young woman, 36 come next Candle-mas Day, white, Irish, who loves to hitch-hike on fire engines in spare time, is anxious to meet a college boy with motorcycle and sea-sled. Would prefer one who doesn't toe in, sing Ramona and throw bottles when displeased.—Arabella.

* * *

Lonely Hearts. Widow with nine-story tenement on East Side would enjoy meeting a man who understands practical plumbing, wall-papering, ash removing and care of furnace. One who knows something about floor varnishing preferred. Good home, steady meals.—Mrs. X.

* * *

Lonely Hearts. Two sisters, Swedish, olive eyes, double chins, nice dispositions, would like to make acquaintance of a young society man who can make shadows, do card tricks, operate magic lantern and read loud from Police Gazette and Iron Age. Must look neat in straw hats and live in America.—Daisy and Moll.

* * *

Lonely Hearts. Home girl who finds most men uninteresting and who is anxious to know a man who doesn't follow the beaten paths and who will show her new phases of life. Must be some one of lofty ambitions, nerve, courage and determination with aptitude for outdoor life. Would consider flagpole sitter or human fly.—Gloria.

49

disguise. Once he put on a suit, tie and spectacles, he was no longer Harry F. Powers—he could be whoever he wanted to be and no one could stop him. The victims were giving him their life's savings and land willingly. The ploy was simple: send for a list of wealthy widows and other vulnerable yet well-to-do victims. Write to them and disclose all sorts of fallacies about his career and financial status. For Lena Fellows, he promised that they would marry quickly in a most beautiful location. The only catch was that she had to drain her bank account and pack her valuables for the trip.

> *Wealthy widower, worth $150,000. Has income from $400 to $2,000 a month. Own a beautiful 10-room brick home, completely furnished with everything that would make a good woman happy. My wife would have her own car and plenty of spending money. Would have nothing to do but enjoy herself.*
> *—ad placed by Powers*

In early 1931, Powers placed the above ad in search of new victims. Along with the ad, he bought the wealthy widows list from the American Friendship Society for $0.02, which garnered nearly one hundred responses from vulnerable women who were ready to open their hearts and bank accounts to him. He listed his profession as a civil engineer and his net worth as $150,000. The women were a most disposable commodity to Powers. They were not human or deserving of respect to him. Instead, they were things to be used and tossed away once they are no longer valuable.

The ads that Powers answered were almost always those placed by women of means and status. The ads that he placed would lead lonely women to believe that he was a man of a certain caliber—high class and rich. In order to pass himself off as such, he used several aliases (according to the Serial Killer Database), including John Schroeder, Joseph Gildow, Harold Bjorgo, D.P. Lowther, A.R. Weaver, Harry F. Powers and Cornelius Orvin Pierson. Also, when answering an ad, he wrote a series of love letters to gain the trust and adoration of his targets. In his letters to prospective victims, Powers mentioned that he was "a Mason who owned a 10-room house." He made promises to purchase cars and provide financial security, only asking in return for loyalty and commitment. Naturally, he received many responses from women seeking his "generosity." He managed to intrigue and correspond with nearly one hundred women.

CRIMINAL PROFILE

A leopard cannot change its spots, nor can a killer change his ways. That's the thing about people who kill—time and again, no matter the date or time in history, the one constant fact is that they will exhibit predatory behavior as a prerequisite to the kill, and if given the opportunity after they kill, they will seize it to kill again. At the time, Powers's crime was called the "most horrible tragedy that [had] taken place in [the] American annals."[15]

What led Harry F. Powers down the dark path of becoming a serial killer? Experts suggest that a combination of childhood trauma, psychological disorders and a deep-seated need for power and control often contribute to killers' murderous tendencies. To understand what made Powers a killer, it is necessary to delve into his twisted psyche and examine the factors that contributed to his heinous crimes.

Powers possessed an insatiable desire for power and control over others. This need for dominance manifested itself through various manipulative tactics, particularly in his pursuit of vulnerable women through lonely hearts advertisements. He preyed on their loneliness and desperation, luring them into his web of deceit with promises of love and companionship. Once they were ensnared, Powers's true sadistic nature emerged.

Powers may have had a predisposition to kill that more than likely evolved from his childhood in the Netherlands and only came to the surface upon arrival to the United States. The combination of possible traumatic experiences in his youth, coupled with his deep-seated need for power and control over others, created the perfect storm for him to become a cold-blooded killer. The darkness that lay within him was unleashed on those unfortunate enough to cross paths with him.

Harry F. Powers derived pleasure from traumatizing his victims. He reveled in the fear and experienced ecstasy from the torture and humiliation of all of his victims. His victims were subjected to unimaginable horrors before meeting their tragic fates at his hands. In the world of psychology, the typology in which this type of killer falls is the hedonistic category. The hedonistic killer experiences sexual pleasure when they commit a murder. Further, their quest for this feeling of pleasure is what drives them to continue to kill. Hedonistic killers fall into three categories: lust-oriented, comfort-oriented and thrill-oriented. The lust-oriented killers get sexual satisfaction out of taking a person's life. They need to be close to their target when they kill and will employ methods of murder involving their hands (such as strangulation, asphyxiation or stabbing). The comfort-oriented killer will kill for material gain but gains no pleasure out of committing the murderous act and more often than not will use poison in order to commit the murder so that they can cash in on insurance policies or inheritance money. Finally, the thrill-oriented killer enjoys the chase of their victim. They get immense pleasure out of seeing the fear in their target's eyes and doing things that create fear. They might stalk their victims, torture them and prolong the events that lead up to the eventual murder. It's not the murder in and of itself that interests this type of killer; it is the fear and pleading of the victim that excites them.

While on the surface, Powers seemed like the comfort type of hedonistic killer (because he killed women for their money), he was actually in the lust-oriented category. This revelation came in part from an alleged statement he made during his confession. As Patterson Smith noted in "The Literature of the American Serial Killer," Powers was alleged to have said that the pleasure of watching his victims perish "beat any cathouse that I was ever in."[16] Additionally, renowned yet controversial anthropologist at the time Dr. Aleš Hrdlička mentioned in an interview that Powers had "an exaggerated lust to kill which dominated his entire personality."[17] He went on to state that the lust to kill was not an indicator of insanity because Powers liked to kill "for killings sake," as evidenced when he killed the children of Asta Eicher. Further, Dr. Hrdlička noted that "the lust to kill was far more powerful than any lust for profit, [as the] lust for profit is incidental."

The interesting thing here is that Dr. Hrdlička likened the lust to kill as being native to animals and even mentioned that this need to kill was prevalent in Neanderthals. Not that Powers was a neanderthal, but it seemed that Dr. Hrdlička was illustrating the need to kill for the sake of killing is an animalistic or primitive construct that goes back to the hunter-gather, predator-prey mindset. The point of the commentary from Dr. Hrdlička was to illustrate that Powers was of sound mind and body when he decided to commit the murders of the women and children.

A psychiatrist (referred to as "alienist" during that time) by the name of Edward Everett Mayer was brought in by the Clarksburg police from the University of Pittsburgh to examine Powers with hopes of discouraging an insanity plea. After speaking with Powers, Dr. Mayer agreed that Powers was not insane and was "capable of knowing right from wrong." Further, Dr. Mayer described Powers as having a "psychopathic personality…[that was] squat, pig-eyed, and paunchy with weakened sexual powers."[18] In short, Powers was well aware of what he was doing and would intentionally lure vulnerable women by telling them what they want to hear, only to lead them promptly to their deaths. Understanding what made Harry F. Powers a killer is not meant to excuse or justify his actions; rather it provides insight into the complex motivations behind such disturbing behavior. By examining these factors, society can better comprehend the depths of human depravity while striving toward prevention and justice.

VICTIM PROFILE

In order to understand the rationale behind Powers selecting the victims that he chose, it is important to understand the profile of the victims. Creating a victim profile for serial killers like Powers can be a complex and multidisciplinary process that involves a careful analysis of available evidence, crime scene characteristics, offender behavior and psychological factors. This process aims to uncover patterns, motives and potential vulnerabilities of victims to aid law enforcement agencies in their investigation. Victim profiling is a critical tool in understanding the mindsets of both offenders and victims, contributing to the development of investigative strategies and preventive measures. Additionally, victim profiling is a subset of criminal profiling, which is the practice of analyzing crime scenes and behavioral patterns to infer characteristics of offenders. It focuses specifically on the traits, behaviors and circumstances of victims, shedding light on why certain individuals become targets of serial killers. Currently, federal agents (profilers in particular) seek to identify commonalities among victims, the motivations of the killer and any potential vulnerabilities that might attract the offender. During the era in which Powers committed his crimes, there were no official federal profilers available—the FBI was in its infancy, and all correspondence about criminals that were "high profile" was sent directly to J. Edgar Hoover.

It is important to note that the characteristics of the crime scene play a vital role in constructing a victim profile. Details such as location, disposal of bodies, choice of location and method of killing can provide insights into the killer's familiarity with the area, level of planning and potential motives. Analyzing victim demographics, such as age, gender, ethnicity and socioeconomic status, helps in identifying patterns that might guide the selection process of victims. Serial killers often have preferences based on these factors, which can reveal aspects of their psychological motives.

Understanding the lifestyle and routines of victims can provide clues about their daily activities, interactions and potential risky behaviors. Serial killers often exploit vulnerabilities in victims' routines to facilitate their crimes. Profilers examine the psychological characteristics of victims, including personality traits, mental health issues and any history of trauma or abuse. These factors can indicate why certain individuals might be targeted or the killer's attempt to exert control over vulnerable victims. Geographic information systems (GIS) are used to analyze the spatial distribution of crime scenes, allowing profilers to predict the offender's base or anchor point. This technique helps narrow down potential areas where the killer might reside.

The motives and fantasies of the serial killer can provide insight into the types of victims targeted. Motives such as power, control and sexual gratification influence the selection process. In the case of Powers, his motives were power, control, financial gain and sexual satisfaction by preying on vulnerable women of means, gaining their trust and then taking their lives with his hands. Serial killers often exhibit signature behaviors—unique elements that distinguish their crimes from others. These behaviors might provide clues about the offender's personality and preferences in victims. Profiling relies heavily on behavioral analysis to infer why an offender selects particular victims. By examining crime scene behaviors, an understanding of the offender's emotional state, level of organization and familiarity with the victim can be derived. Behaviors such as postmortem mutilation or posing of bodies provide insight into the killer's psychological motivations. Victim profiling can be either predictive or descriptive. Predictive profiling aims to identify potential future victims and inform preventive measures. Descriptive profiling seeks to understand past victims to aid in apprehending the offender. Both approaches draw from similar factors but have different applications.

Nearly all of Powers's victims were Caucasian women who were either widowed or single. Additionally, the female victims had either amassed a small fortune or had a rather attractive savings account. In the late 1920s and early 1930s, an unmarried woman who was middle-aged was considered a spinster. For many women, marriage provided not only security but a chance to align themselves with a good reputation as well. During this time in American history, marriage was considered an accomplishment for women, and marriage to a man of means was considered a major feat. A quick glance at the victims reveals that both had dark hair, were single and near middle age. The children were casualties who were killed to satisfy the deep-seated desire that Powers had to kill. Both women had a small savings account, and both were looking for love with the "right" man. Neither woman was taller than Powers, nor were they stronger than him. He made sure to study them—seeking out their vulnerabilities, which they voluntarily revealed in their letters to him.

The victims were simply women who fell prey to his cunning and manipulative ways. Each one had a certain naivete that surrounded her hopes and dreams of companionship, love and happiness. Sadly, they would never have the chance to see them fulfilled. The stories of Powers's victims serve as a sobering reminder that evil can exist even in seemingly ordinary places like small towns in West Virginia.

THE VICTIMS

There are more people starving for love and companionship than there are starving for bread.
—taken from a 1931 ad from the American Friendship Society of Detroit

Women were easy prey for both murderers and the American Friendship Society. After all, the society offered free lists of the names of wealthy widows to anybody who could pay two cents for them. Asta Eicher was one of those widows, and Dorothy Lemke was as well. While they were the only women who were reported to be murdered by Powers and whose names were printed on the list provided by the American Friendship Society, they were not the only women on the list who were contacted and targeted by him. They were merely the first two women that he had admitted to killing.

Asta Eicher

Asta Bothilde Christensen Eicher (often referred to as Asta Bothilde Buick in contemporary accounts) was born in 1881 in Copenhagen, Denmark. Asta and her mother, Anna Larsen, sailed on the SS *Helig Olav* from Denmark to the United States on July 25, 1907. At the time, Asta's mother was a widow. Public record notes that Asta married Heinrich "Henri" Anton Eicher on April 30, 1908. Henri was born in Zurich, Switzerland, in 1876, and immigrated to the United States from Denmark on the SS *Helig Olav* from Denmark on June 13, 1907.

By 1909, Henri had taken over as manager of the Kalo Shop's silversmiths, and he also had a workshop in his Park Ridge garage and barn where he and the other Kalo silversmiths worked in their spare time. The barn/workshop also served as a place where the Randahl Shop and the Volund Shop were founded. On August 21, 1913, Henri became a naturalized citizen, and by 1915, he owned and operated his own company, H.A. Eicher, out of the barn as well.

Notably, Henri was one of the Kalo Shop's first silversmiths and foremen. His sterling silver trays, silverware and dinnerware are considered some of the best in the region and premiered in or around 1915–23. Henri, Asta and her mother lived at a beautiful home on 312 Cedar Street, a two-story frame house with a front gable. The house is one of the oldest in Park Ridge, having been constructed in 1835. There are two of the original outbuildings still standing on the property, a chicken coop and a tiny barn that Eicher used as a workshop. A brief look at Zillow or Redfin indicates that the house is lovely, complete with a beautiful tree in the front and four bedrooms and 2,093 square feet of living space, perfect for a growing family.

Because of Henri's accomplishments, the Eichers became well known in Park Ridge. In addition to cufflinks and other tiny jewelry pieces, he was well known for his sterling silver tea and coffee utensils, water pitchers, fluted bowls, salad servers, bread trays and vases. The silver chalice at St. Mary's Catholic Church in Park Ridge is credited to him as well. In 1916, his eldest daughter, Grete Lillian, was born. Henri then hired a manufacturer's representative to distribute his wares to jewelry stores and boutiques around the country, and his work was prominently displayed in a showroom in Chicago's Heyworth Building. By the latter half of the summer of 1918, Asta had buried her mother, and in midwinter of 1919, she gave birth to her son, Harry Anthony. Henri managed to create wares until in or around 1919, when he was diagnosed with mental illness. In 1920, his youngest daughter, Annabel, was born, and with her birth came joy and a revitalization of happiness in the home. However, three years later, according to public record, Henri succumbed to complications surrounding his mental illness in Cook County on August 12, 1923. Asta was now a widow, alone with three small children.

After Henri's passing, Asta became the executor of his estate and manager of his businesses. She was successful in negotiating the silverwork of her husband and a few loyal silversmiths on commission for the Kalo Shop until 1931, when she was forced to close the studio. She was accustomed to leading a comfortable life, and because she already had children, she looked for a husband who could provide a lifestyle that was comparable to the one she had with Henri.

Asta's search for a new spouse led her to meet Powers, who posed as Cornelius Pierson, a wealthy businessman who shared her desire for a lavish lifestyle. Powers, with his charming demeanor and convincing lies, managed to deceive Asta and her children into believing that he was the perfect match. Little did they know that behind his façade of wealth and success, Powers had sinister intentions that would shatter their hopes, dreams and lives altogether. Asta and Powers corresponded for a while, and then one day, out of the blue, Asta announced to her friends that she was starting a new life. At the same time, she asked her boarder, William O'Boyle, to find another place to live. The only insight that she gave her friends about this mystery man was his name: Cornelius Pierson. Soon after, Asta and the children disappeared.

Grethe Lillian, Harry Anthony and Annabel Eicher

July 5, 1931, is a most significant date. Sure, it is the day after our country's Independence Day. It may even be the birthdate of many people worldwide, but in the context of this story, it is the day that three innocent children lost their lives. It is the day that Harry F. Powers heinously murdered the Eicher children.

While not much is known about the children, it can be assumed that, like most children of the time, they were excited at the chance of a new beginning with their mother in a new place. Grethe was fourteen years old, Harry was twelve years old and Annabel was nine years old at the time. They had likely been looking forward to exploring their new surroundings, making new friends and starting afresh. However, their dreams were brutally shattered on that fateful day. More than likely, they were terrified, having to reconcile that their mother had been murdered by Powers ten days prior, on June 25, 1931. They couldn't comprehend the heinous act that had taken away their loving mother. The shock and grief must have overwhelmed them, leaving them feeling lost and abandoned in a world that suddenly seemed cruel and unpredictable. They were left with a void that could never be filled, and the pain of their loss seemed insurmountable. The fear that consumed them must have been unbearable. On arrival to West Virginia, they were not greeted by their loving mother and kind neighbors. Instead, they were rushed through a trapdoor in the garage with a stairwell that led to a subterranean chamber of cells with concrete walls. They were all alone, horrified and suffering in the darkness and deafening silence of the chamber. The last time that they saw a shimmer of light was when Powers opened the trapdoor to guide them one at a time to the noose that he affixed around their necks before strangling them, watching with quiet elation as they struggled for air and then finally took their last breath.

It would be nearly fifty-five days before law enforcement found the four secret rooms where the children were detained and murdered. And as time would have it, the police would also find the bloody footprint of a child, a burned bankbook, blood-soaked hair and clothing that they once wore.

Dorothy Lemke

Dorothy Pressler Lemke was a widow who resided in Northborough, Massachusetts. A nurse by trade, Dorothy, like most nurses, had a penchant for fixing people. It wouldn't be too far-fetched to think that Dorothy ignored the signs when it came to Powers and instead thought that with a little devotion she could fix his undesirable traits.

During Powers's later trial, a man by the name of Ed Kemper testified that he received a withdrawal request from Lemke's bank account on August 1, 1931. He had held the position of assistant cashier at the Second National Bank in Uniontown, Pennsylvania, since March 1, 1931. During the trial, Kemper reviewed the bank record and mentioned that on July 28, 1931, a man resembling Powers had brought a check from the Worcester County Institution for Savings for the amount of $2,754.22 payable to Dorothy Lemke yet endorsed by an "A.R. Weaver." A second check was presented for payment in the amount of $1,533.01 also endorsed by "A.R. Weaver," but this one was made payable to "Dorothy Pressler." Kemper further testified that the man who was brought to his office was "short, heavyset and wore a gray suit and matching felt hat." The prosecution argued that these transactions provided clear evidence of Powers's intent to commit fraud and established a motive for his involvement in the murder of Dorothy Lemke.

The cross-examination from Powers's attorney J.E. Law attempted to discredit the witness but could not do so because Kemper recollected that Powers returned to the bank on August 7, 1931, attempting to cash the checks and then again on August 10, 1931. Kemper admitted that the teller on duty, Wallace H. Teets, brought Powers back to his office on August 1 and August 7, but he did not personally see him on August 10. Despite not personally seeing Powers on August 10, Kemper's testimony still provided strong evidence against him. The fact that Powers attempted to cash the checks on multiple occasions after Dorothy Lemke's disappearance raised suspicions about his involvement. Teets testified that there was a specific process for receiving payment on checks drawn from accounts at the bank. It included a "direct straight to the bank" collection from Worcester, Massachusetts, and then the bank sent a New York draft for each of the checks presented made payable to Second National Bank at Uniontown. Teets added that Powers was at the window of another teller with the checks, and when that teller did not have enough money to pay him at her window, Powers was sent down to him. At that time, Teets asked a few questions regarding the checks due to their unusual size. He asked Powers where he got them; further, he asked if Powers wanted to deposit the checks or if he wanted them to be cashed. Powers expressed wanting cash. There was a conversational exchange between Teets and Kemper about the checks prior to Teets telling Powers that he would need to return in a few days.

A defendant named R. Glenn Crawford was called to the stand to testify about the checks. He was a bookkeeper for Empire National Bank. At the time, banks assigned bookkeepers to maintain ledgers for clients whose last names were arranged in groups. Crawford was assigned clients whose names ended in *L* through *S*. Crawford noted that "H.F. Powers" had an account with Empire National Bank. He further noted that he recognized Powers's handwriting and signature. During his testimony, he noted that the account owned by Powers received a deposit on August 11, 1931, in the amount of $2,000.00. The account was credited for that same amount on August 21, 1931. Shortly thereafter, Powers presented a series of deposits and then closed the account when he deposited a check in the amount of $3,657.63.

The defense's attempt to discredit the witness proved unsuccessful, further strengthening the case against Powers. These details painted a damning picture of Powers's motive and potential guilt in the murder of Dorothy Lemke. The prosecution presented a compelling argument that suggested Powers had a clear motive to harm Lemke. They highlighted Powers's patterns of targeting well-to-do, lonely widows and the fact that Lemke was both a widow and had a substantial amount of money in the bank. The prosecution argued that Powers saw an opportunity to gain more money by eliminating Lemke and claiming her funds. The combination of the testimony of the cashier, teller and accountant as well as the motive presented by the prosecution left little doubt in the minds of the jury about Powers's potential guilt in the heinous crime. Not to mention, at this time, most of the money in Powers's account belonged to Lemke.

HARRY F. POWERS ON THE DARK TRIAD

The dark personality triad refers to a constellation of three distinct but interrelated personality traits: narcissism, Machiavellianism and psychopathy. These traits, when present at high levels in an individual, can give rise to malevolent, manipulative and callous behaviors that can cause harm to others and disrupt social cohesion.

The term *narcissism* is derived from the Greek myth of Narcissus, who fell in love with his reflection. This trait is characterized by an inflated sense of self-importance, a deep need for excessive attention and admiration and a lack of empathy for others. Individuals with high levels of narcissism often feel superior and may engage in grandiose fantasies. Their self-centeredness can lead to exploitative behaviors, especially when they perceive that their ego is threatened.

Machiavellianism is named after the Italian Renaissance writer Niccolò Machiavelli, who penned *The Prince*. Machiavellianism is characterized by a duplicitous interpersonal style, a cynical disregard for morality and a focus on personal gain and power. Personality traits also include superficial charm, manipulativeness and lack of remorse. These traits create a potent mix that makes certain individuals particularly dangerous. Highly Machiavellian individuals are pragmatic, focused on their own interests, and often employ deceit to achieve their goals. They are strategic in their interpersonal dealings and often view others as mere tools to be used.

Psychopathy is perhaps the most unsettling of the triad. It is characterized by a chronic antisocial behavior; diminished empathy and remorse; and bold, disinhibited and egotistical traits. Psychopaths might engage in behaviors that are harmful to others without feeling guilt or remorse. Their charm can be superficial, serving as a mask to exploit and harm others.

Powers, with his cold and calculated method of luring victims through matrimonial ads, most distinctly typifies the traits associated with psychopathy. His actions demonstrate a severe lack of empathy and remorse. The systematic manner in which he deceived, exploited and then killed his victims indicates a high level of cunning and strategic thinking, which is also consistent with Machiavellianism. While one could argue that his actions might have been driven by a need for financial gain or even twisted pleasure, the ruthlessness and detachment with which he operated resonate strongly with the characteristics of psychopathy.

THE DEPTHS OF HUMAN DEPRAVITY

Understanding the motivations behind men who kill women and children for financial gain requires an understanding of various societal, psychological and economic factors. Poverty, desperation and a lack of opportunities may drive individuals to engage in illicit activities. Men who have personalities on the dark triad (Machiavellianism, narcissism and psychopathy) may perceive violence as a means to obtain wealth or maintain status, using women and children as pawns in their destructive pursuit.

The psychological profile of men like Powers who perpetrate such heinous acts as killing women and children for financial gain highlights the distorted thinking and moral decay present in these individuals. Factors like a history of trauma, mental illness or a distorted sense of power and control can contribute to the development of a mindset that justifies the taking of innocent and vulnerable lives. The dehumanization of women and children further fuels the dark impulses that drive these men to commit unimaginable acts.

The capacity for malevolence within the human psyche remains one of the most perplexing and haunting aspects of our nature. Throughout history, instances of extreme cruelty and wickedness have repeatedly emerged, giving testament to the depths of human depravity. These acts, perpetrated by individuals, groups or even entire societies, challenge fundamental beliefs about human goodness and the place people have in the universe. The darkness within the human species is juxtaposed against the ability to love, create and aspire, making its existence all the more confounding.

Powers, among others, exemplifies this perplexing malevolence. He was a seemingly ordinary man who was originally from the Netherlands but posed as a West Virginia businessman in the early twentieth century and used matrimonial advertisements to lure unsuspecting victims, primarily women and children, into his web of deceit. Once he had gained their trust, he would rob them of their money and take their lives, discarding them as if they held no intrinsic value. The motivations behind such acts are difficult to fathom. To kill for personal gain, especially in such a cold, calculated manner, goes beyond the bounds of what most consider human. It forces us to confront the terrifying possibility that within the spectrum of human behavior, there exists a range of actions from the most virtuous to the utterly vile. Further, it forces people to accept the true horror that human beings can be the deadliest of predators on the entire earth.

What drives men like Powers? Is it a unique blend of nature and nurture, a perfect storm of circumstances that creates such monsters? Or is there a dormant darkness within us all, kept in check only by societal norms, personal ethics and fear of consequence? Theories abound, from psychological disorders to societal influences, yet no single explanation suffices. The existence of such individuals serves as a stark reminder that, alongside our capacity for compassion, creativity and love, there lurks a potential for unspeakable evil. It underscores the importance of vigilance, both in safeguarding our societies and in understanding the vast complexities of the human condition.

3

THE CRIME

There was deception on the horizon and murder in the wind in the summer of 1931. The cruel irony was that the fate of the Eicher family (among other victims) was written in blood. Harry F. Powers began building a garage in the latter part of the previous year. It was a project that looked odd yet harmless to the residents of Quiet Dell. As he put the finishing touches on the garage, all seemed well on the home front. According to a witness who saw him build the garage, "Powers worked diligently and seemed focused on completing the project efficiently." The witness also mentioned that Powers appeared to be in good spirits and interacted politely with neighbors during the construction process. However, Powers did not construct his "murder garage" alone. Instead, he actively sought out the assistance of people who lived near the property, many of whom he solicited to dig ditches for sewer pipes (as they were told) that would go from the garage to a small estuary named Elk Creek. It was along these sewer pipes where a victim would be found.

> *They took it quietly.*
> *—Harry F. Powers (in response to how the victims responded to his treachery and torture)*

Those were the words that Powers used when he told the police about the last moments of each of his victims—*they took it* quietly—as if murder was something a human being could welcome gingerly. *They took it quietly…*

when his hands gradually tightened around their necks...*they took it quietly*... when both women were locked in the dark and musty stalls of his murder garage...*they took it quietly*...when he tortured them one by one and made the children watch the hammer fall hard against the head of the second-oldest child and only boy. *They took it quietly*, when he reached a sexual climax while fracturing the U-shaped hyoid bones of the women and female children. But the quiet was not the only component of the torture, as his victims were indeed tortured and starved for days prior to their untimely demise. The torment inflicted on his victims extended beyond the physical pain and suffering. He derived a sick pleasure from their helplessness, relishing in the psychological torture he imposed on them. The darkness of his murder garage served as a haunting backdrop to the unimaginable horrors that unfolded within its walls.

When questioned by police, Powers provided an entirely different account. His account included a road trip that began in Illinois, where he allegedly picked up Asta Eicher and her three children (Greta, Harry and Annabel); passed through Massachusetts, where he allegedly picked up Dorothy Lemke; and ended in Quiet Dell, West Virginia. Powers claimed that during the road trip, they had all been enjoying one another's company and engaging in pleasantries, which was strange because even back then it would be nearly impossible for two women involved with the same man to truly get along, let alone enjoy a road trip together. Powers, however, insisted that there was no sign of any malicious intentions or any indication of the psychological torture he was later accused of inflicting on them. But the court records provided a more sinister account of the events immediately preceding the deaths of Eicher, Lemke and the children. But what actually happened is that in late June 1931 he drove to Illinois to pick up Asta and took her to Quiet Dell, West Virginia, where he murdered her in the garage that he had built only two months prior.

The children were left under the care of a family friend named Elizabeth Abernathy in Park Ridge, Illinois. After a few days had passed, Abernathy got a letter from Asta instructing her to release the children to Powers, as she was sending him to pick them up so they could be reunited for a fresh start in West Virginia. Although it seemed a bit out of character, Abernathy did not question it and gave the children to Powers. From that point, Powers took the children back to West Virginia but tried to cash a forged check at the bank first. On arriving in West Virginia, Powers locked the children up in the garage and starved them. The garage was built so that no one could hear what happened in the subterranean region, where he left the children alone and captive. He had no use for them, unfortunately, and decided that since the children were not an asset to his plan, he had no other recourse but to kill them, which he did ten days after he killed their mother. Powers believed that by eliminating the children, he would erase any potential witnesses to his crimes. With a cold and calculated heart, he carried out his sinister act, thinking that he left no trace of their existence. The darkness that engulfed the subterranean chamber in the garage was a chilling testament to the depths of his depravity, forever haunting the memories of those who would come to uncover this horrifying truth.

> *"I was permitting little Harry Eicher to watch the killing of his mother and the others, but in the middle of it he let out an awful scream," Powers told police. "I was afraid the neighbors would hear it, so I picked up a hammer and let him have it."*
> *—Harry F. Powers on the murder of the Eicher family and Dorothy Lemke*

It all started with an ad, followed by a letter promising a new life for the widow Eicher and her children. The ad had offered them a chance to escape their current hardships and find solace in a close-knit community. Intrigued by the promise of a fresh start, Eicher reached out and expressed her interest in the opportunity. Little did she know that this seemingly hopeful beginning would lead to a series of tragic events that would forever change their lives.

The crime unfolded rather quickly. After corresponding with Asta Eicher and gaining her trust, Powers visited her. It is believed that he persuaded or coerced her into giving him access to her financial resources. After obtaining her money, Powers murdered Eicher and later her children.

When the police investigated his activities, they found that financial deception was a common thread in his interactions with victims. He would use matrimonial advertisements to lure lonely women, gain their trust and then rob them before killing them. Asta Eicher was one of these tragic victims. Powers was a cunning and manipulative predator who preyed on vulnerable individuals seeking companionship. Asta Eicher, a kind-hearted and trusting woman, fell victim to his deceitful tactics. Unbeknownst to her, Powers had a sinister plan to exploit her financially and ultimately end her life, leaving a trail of devastation in his wake. The investigation into Powers's activities revealed a chilling pattern, exposing him as a merciless killer who used trust as a weapon to satisfy his sinister desires. Powers would carefully choose his victims, selecting those who were lonely and desperate for love. He would charm and manipulate them, gaining their trust and affection before revealing his true intentions. As the investigation continued, it became clear that Asta was not his only victim. Powers had left a trail of broken hearts and shattered lives behind him, each one a testament to his cold-hearted nature and his ability to exploit the vulnerabilities of others. The revelation of his true identity sent shockwaves through the community, leaving everyone questioning who they could truly trust.

In many accounts, it is said that he killed Asta, then Annabel, then Harry and left Grethe for last—as evidenced by a letter to the eldest girl from Powers. It appeared to be a ploy in which he may have been trying to get her to let her guard down. Although the letter looked like he may have been grooming the young girl as well. Additionally, Powers hit Harry in the head with a hammer. He mentioned that it was because Harry screamed and he was afraid that the neighbors would hear the crime being committed. The issue here is that Powers was a bona fide criminal, and by the time he'd begun killing the Eichers, he'd already strangled Lemke and buried her. In short, he was no stranger to murder. He actually enjoyed watching the terror and fear in the eyes of his victims and admitted as such to the police when he likened the feeling of taking the lives of his victims to the feeling a man might get when engaging in the services of the prostitutes in a cathouse or brothel. In lieu of this, it is hard to believe that while Powers strangled Asta, Harry screamed and then Powers stopped strangling Asta to pick up a hammer and strike young Harry in the head to prevent him from screaming. While possible, it does not seem plausible. If anything, a killer like Powers more than likely struck young Harry on the side of his head at another time and took reverie in the moment that the hammer striking the child's head resulted in the loss of life. That's the type of killer that Powers was—the sort that thoroughly enjoyed the power that came with taking the life of a human being. There was an element of sadism to his murders, for with the Eicher family, he had driven them from Chicago, Illinois, to his farm and left them locked in subterranean chambers to starve while he continued his criminal activities. Upon his return, he hanged them one by one, except for Harry (the boy), whom he struck with a hammer on the side of his head.

Prior to the murder of Asta Eicher and her children, Powers murdered Dorothy Lemke by strangling her. He then stuffed her body in a burlap bag and buried her remains near the sewage pipe on the property that he shared with his wife. Much like Eicher, Lemke was convinced that she'd married the love of her life and fully trusted Powers. In July 1931, Lemke left Northborough, Massachusetts, and ended up in Iowa with Powers. The two were married and then set off for Quiet Dell, West Virginia. That's when the trail went cold for Lemke. The discovery of her remains shook the community to its core, as they realized the depth of Powers's deception and the extent of his brutal actions. It became evident that he had been methodically preying on vulnerable women for years, leaving a trail of death and destruction in his wake. The revelation not only shattered the trust of those who had once considered him a friend but also instilled a deep sense of fear and unease among the residents, knowing that evil could lurk behind the façade of anyone they knew.

But why did he kill? It was due in part to a feeling that he craved—an insatiable hunger inside of him that would reveal its insidious head always encouraging him to commit the unspeakable crime of murder. It was something, like most killers, he felt he had to do. There was no moral code that stopped him—there was no right or wrong—just a continuum, a gray space where the urge lay patiently, waiting to be fulfilled through the execution of his next victim. During the commission of his crimes, he experienced orgasmic highs driven by the need to exterminate his victims.

4

THE CAPTURE

Police Findings and Media Coverage

After the disappearance of Asta Eicher and her children in Park Ridge, Illinois, suspicions arose. Neighbors and friends had noticed Powers rummaging through the Eicher home. Powers gave the explanation that Eicher had gone to Europe and he was looking after her affairs, but some did not find his story convincing. They couldn't help but recall the menacing aura that surrounded Powers, his cold and calculating eyes that seemed to pierce through one's soul, and so they notified the police of the missing children and Eicher herself. As the investigation into the disappearance progressed, more unsettling details came to light—Powers's criminal record, his troubled past and his uncanny ability to manipulate those around him. The once close-knit community now lived in constant fear as a result of the realization that evil had indeed been hiding behind the smile of someone they had once trusted. It was a chilling reminder that darkness can lurk even in the most familiar faces. Paranoid whispers echoed through the streets. The once vibrant town had transformed into a ghostly shell as residents grappled with the horrifying truth that evil had woven its way into their lives. Authorities began to look into the mysterious Cornelius O. Pierson (one of the aliases used by Powers) after finding letters from him with postage and handling from Clarksburg, West Virginia, in Eicher's home.

This led the authorities to Powers's residence in Quiet Dell, West Virginia. On searching his property, authorities made the gruesome discovery of multiple bodies buried in the garage, including those of Eicher and her children. They also found the remains of other victims, revealing the extent of Powers's heinous crimes. The investigation into Powers's crimes uncovered a chilling pattern of luring vulnerable women through personal ads and preying on their trust. It became evident that Powers had meticulously planned and executed these horrific acts, leaving a trail of devastation in his wake. The investigation uncovered a terrifying web of deception and manipulation, as Powers had lured his victims through charm and promises of a better life. It became apparent that Powers had carefully planned his crimes, creating false identities, using them to gain trust, and often visiting the women he'd contacted prior to seizing the opportunity to take his victim's lives. The shocking revelations sent shockwaves through the small community of Quiet Dell and the nation at large. The once innocent notion of seeking love or companionship now seemed like a treacherous gamble, causing people to question the intentions of those they met. The chilling story of Powers left a lasting scar on the collective consciousness, forever altering the way people approached relationships and embedding a sense of caution and skepticism in their hearts.

FROM INVESTIGATION TO CONVICTION: ANALYZING THE ROLE OF LAW ENFORCEMENT AND J. EDGAR HOOVER IN THE HARRY F. POWERS CASE

The investigation process in the Harry F. Powers case was profoundly influenced by Hoover's leadership and guidance. The Powers case

Harry Powers mug shot, 1931.
Newspapers.com.

Above: *Daily News*, September 1, 1931. *Newspapers.com*.

Opposite: *Sunday News*, front page, 1931. *Newspapers.com*.

witnessed the establishment of task forces and specialized units, an effective strategy that streamlined the investigation.[19] The investigation into the Harry F. Powers case involved the active participation of multiple law enforcement agencies at the federal, state and local levels. It was necessary to coordinate efforts across jurisdictions and unite resources, expertise and intelligence to apprehend Powers and put an end to his reign of terror.

The investigation into Powers's crimes presented challenges due to his operations across multiple states. Federal agencies like the Federal Bureau of Investigation (FBI) collaborated closely with state-level entities and local law enforcement, including police departments and sheriffs' offices. This collaboration allowed for effective information sharing, resource allocation and manpower coordination, ultimately leading to the capture of Powers. Crucial to the collaborative effort was the exchange of intelligence and resources among the involved law enforcement agencies. They established communication channels and protocols to swiftly disseminate crucial findings and leads to all relevant parties. By combining their resources and working together, these agencies conducted a comprehensive investigation that left no stone unturned in the pursuit of justice. The investigation into the Powers case went beyond collecting physical evidence. Law enforcement agencies actively sought and secured witnesses and testimonies, ensuring cooperation from key individuals with crucial information. This aspect of the investigation was vital in building a strong case against Powers and presenting a comprehensive and compelling narrative in court.

There is no passion so contagious as that of fear.
—Michel de Montaigne

The fear and mistrust that permeated Quiet Dell in the aftermath of the killings was palpable. Neighbors who had once exchanged friendly greetings now regarded one another with wary eyes, wondering if behind the smiles and pleasantries lurked a hidden darkness. The town became a fortress of locked doors and drawn curtains as people sought to protect themselves from the potential dangers that lay outside. Even in the wider world, the tale of Powers and his heinous crimes served as a cautionary tale, a reminder that evil could be lurking in the most unexpected places. No longer could anyone blindly trust another's intentions or take their friendly demeanor at face value. Doubt and paranoia seeped into every interaction, leaving a lingering sense of unease that tainted the once warm and welcoming atmosphere of the town. The darkness that had been exposed had forever changed the way people viewed their surroundings, forever altering the fabric of their once peaceful existence.

Public outrage over the case was immense, given the nature of his crimes and the fact that he preyed on lonely women seeking companionship. After

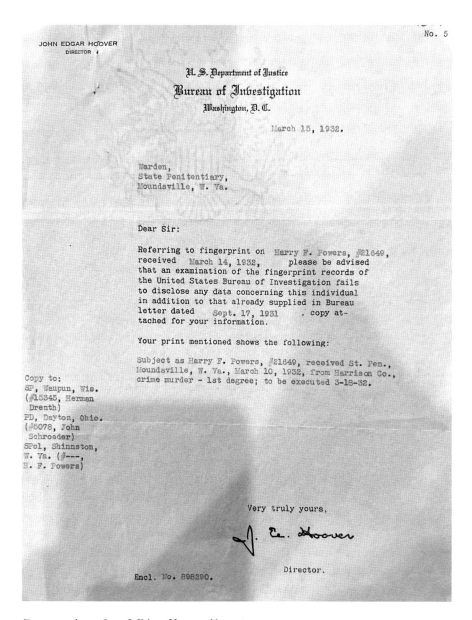

JOHN EDGAR HOOVER
DIRECTOR

U. S. Department of Justice

Bureau of Investigation

Washington, D. C.

March 15, 1932.

Warden,
State Penitentiary,
Moundsville, W. Va.

Dear Sir:

Referring to fingerprint on Harry F. Powers, #21649, received March 14, 1932, please be advised that an examination of the fingerprint records of the United States Bureau of Investigation fails to disclose any data concerning this individual in addition to that already supplied in Bureau letter dated Sept. 17, 1931, copy attached for your information.

Your print mentioned shows the following:

Subject as Harry F. Powers, #21649, received St. Pen., Moundsville, W. Va., March 10, 1932, from Harrison Co., crime murder - 1st degree; to be executed 3-18-32.

Copy to:
SP, Waupun, Wis.
(#15345, Herman
Drenth)
PD, Dayton, Ohio.
(#5078, John
Schroeder)
SPol, Shinnston,
W. Va. (#---,
H. F. Powers)

Very truly yours,

J. E. Hoover

Director.

Encl. No. 898290.

Correspondence from J. Edgar Hoover. *Newspapers.com.*

his arrest, Powers confessed to his crimes. The community was shaken to its core as they realized that this monster had been living among them, disguising his sinister intentions with charm and charisma. The knowledge that their neighbors, friends and even family members could harbor such darkness sparked a deep mistrust that now hung heavily in the air. Everyone became more cautious, constantly questioning the true intentions of those around them, fearful of who could be the next hidden predator roaming their quiet streets. The once close-knit bonds that held the town together were broken, replaced with a palpable tension that refused to dissipate.

Nearly one hundred letters were found in the residence of Harry F. Powers They were addressed from women across the nation, one of whom he had already married in another state. All the while, his wife, Luella, and her sister played oblivious to it all. The discovery of these letters shed light on the widespread deception of Harry F. Powers and exposed the shocking extent of his crimes. It became evident that Powers had been leading a double life, preying on vulnerable women and exploiting their trust. The fact that his wife, Luella, and her sister remained unaware of his sinister activities serves as a stark reminder of the hidden darkness that can lurk behind seemingly normal façades. Despite the evidence staring them in the face, neither Luella nor her sister seemed to suspect anything awry in Powers's behavior. Their unwavering ignorance painted a disturbing picture of the power a manipulative individual like Powers could wield over their loved ones. It was a chilling reminder that evil can thrive right under our noses, camouflaged within the normalcy of everyday life. The discovery of Powers's true nature sent shockwaves through the community, leaving everyone questioning what other secrets might be lurking behind closed doors.

It didn't take long for the police to connect the dots. Through working with other police departments in Illinois and Iowa as well as consulting with then director of the Federal Bureau of Investigation J. Edgar Hoover, they were able to put the pieces together as to how and why the crimes were committed. As news of the "Lonely Hearts Killer" spread, law enforcement agencies across the state collaborated in their efforts to apprehend Powers. They meticulously combed through evidence, piecing together a disturbing puzzle that connected numerous disappearances to this enigmatic predator. It was a chilling realization that Powers had been able to deceive the community for so long. In their pursuit of justice, investigators followed leads that led them from one crime scene to another. The trail grew colder with each passing day, but they refused to give up on bringing this deranged killer down.

After weeks of tireless work and relentless determination, authorities closed in on Powers. With precise coordination and careful planning, they were able to trap him within his own web of deceit. The capture of Harry F. Powers marked a significant victory for law enforcement and served as a

SUNDAY NEWS, AUGUST 30, 1931 3

BLUEBEARD ADMITS KILLING 4;
BODY OF 5TH VICTIM FOUND

Harry F. Powers, mail order Bluebeard, confessed murderer of four, now charged with killing another woman.

Stock in trade of a mail order Bluebeard—love letters by which Powers lured Mrs. Asta Eicher to her death.

Cop searches Mrs. Eicher's furniture, piled in garage by Powers so he could rent her home after her murder.

Bluebeard's first victim, the late Mrs. Asta Buick Eicher, killed with her three children by her mail order lover.

Would-Be Bride Seizes Mansion as Scion Flees

Greenwich, Conn., Aug. 29.—Miss Effie Benedict Rhamlow, 33, interior decorator, held possession of the Frederick M. Livingston mansion here today, armed with a marriage license she had just obtained to wed Hendrick Livingston, 24, scion of the household.

Young Mr. Livingston was interviewed about the family's abandonment of the old homestead, as he emerged stealthily from the postern gate with his brother, Freddie, bound for the Berkshires.

Never Will He Wed Her.

"There I shall stay until that woman leaves our roof," said young Mr. Livingston. "Never, never, never will I marry her."

Apprised by a disapproving butler that Hendrick had fled, Miss Rhamlow eyed her marriage license with the sort of glint that would leaped into the eyes of her distinguished Colonial ancestor when they went into battle with the British.

"I am going to stay right here until that man comes back and marries me," said Miss Rhamlow. "Or else—"

Just what prompted Miss Rhamlow to go the Town Hall and get the license was a matter on which

most of Greenwich Society was speculating tonight.

When she got it, according to Miss Nora Murphy, town clerk, she was blushing like the bride she expected to be, and was so reticent about giving the details necessary to filling in the document that Miss Murphy had to prompt her.

It had been known to quite a few, of course, that Miss Rhamlow had been called in some time ago by the Livingstons to redecorate, but none had suspected the remotest possibility of a romance.

It was broken to young Livingston while he was in the midst of a tennis game, with the result that his opponent won a love set.

So He'll Wire Parents.

"It must be a joke," he said. "Why, I've never even held the woman's hand."

But on being assured that it wasn't a funny matter to Miss Rhamlow, Hendrick promptly went into conference with his brother, and both went home and packed.

"I will wire my parents immediately at their Bar Harbor lodge, and let them come down and handle the situation," he added, when safely out of Wylde Manor. "Meanwhile my destination is the Berkshires."

Broker's Auto Pyre Called Camouflage in His Suicide

The police report on the death of Frederick Bender, wealthy retired Park Avenue investment broker, was officially changed yesterday from "accident" to "suicide," when an autopsy revealed that Bender had swallowed potassium cyanide prior to being burned in his automobile Thursday morning.

Following this discovery by city toxicologist, Dr. Alexander O. Gettler, subpoenas were issued yesterday for members of the dead man's family, the fire-lieutenant and patrolman who pulled Bender's body from the blazing machine, and Dr. Roth of Fordham Hospital.

Clew in Empty Vial.

Assistant District Attorney Sylvester Ryan of the Bronx said he wished to question all concerned

Burned auto in which Frederick Bender was killed.

in the case, but told newspaper reporters there were no indications the broker had died by violence.

Bender was found lying across the hood of his blazing auto at Baychester Ave. and 233d St.

(Continued on page 11)

Fiend Cowers in Cell as Crowd Cries Out for Vengeance

By GENEVIEVE HERRICK.

(Special to The Sunday News.)

CLARKSBURG, W. Va., Aug. 29.—After Harry F. Powers, alias Cornelius Pierson, modern Bluebeard, had confessed late today to the murder of Mrs. Asta Buick Eicher, Park Ridge, Ill., widow, and her three children, whose bodies were found in a tunnel under a garage he built in the nearby village of Quiet Dell, the body of another woman was dug from another makeshift grave under the garage. This brought Bluebeard Powers' known victims to five.

First reports were that three more bodies had been found, but the authorities, perhaps in an effort to placate the mob which was demanding the lynching of Powers, made a statement that the other two bodies were "merely logs."

Ex-Sheriff Joseph L. Flannagan, who led the digging party, said, however, that the spades of the workers had

Crowd surrounds ditch leading from Powers' garage in Clarksburg, W. Va., where he buried his five victims.

turned up several pieces of burlap beneath the spot where the fifth body was found, and since all of the other bodies were found encased in this material, Flannagan believes they may find other bodies when the digging is resumed tomorrow.

The possibility that the newly found body may be that of Miss or Mrs. Dorothy Louther or Tressler or Lemke, of either Worcester or Northboro, Mass., was advanced by the local authorities. A trunk of effects belonging to Miss Louther was discovered earlier in the day in a town garage owned and used by Powers. Near the body was found the fragments of a burned bankbook and bank receipts from

covered in his cell where earlier he had made his gruesome confession.

"There are no more bodies," he kept insisting.

At 4 minutes to 4, after hours of police grilling and sobbing out repentence and fear to a minister, Powers, a sniffling creature in a cold sweat of excitement, raised his right hand an swore that the following statement is true.

"My name is Harry F. Powers, alias Cornelius Pierson. I did in the month of July, 1931, murder Mrs. Asta Eicher and three children, Greta, Harry and Annabel, by using a hangman' or strangulation; and I further state that my wife and sister-in-law knew nothing of my plan and are innocent of any—

(Continued on page 4, col. 1)

The net paid circulation for July exceeded

Daily - - - 1,310,000
Sunday - 1,690,000

The Largest Daily and Sunday Circulation in America

the Mechanics Savings Bank of Worcester.

When the news of the latest find was made known to Powers he

Sunday News, August 31, 1931. Newspapers.com.

testament to their unwavering commitment to protecting society from those who would prey on the vulnerable.

The investigation into Powers's crimes was no easy task. With little technology at their disposal in the 1930s, law enforcement had to rely heavily on traditional investigative techniques and witness testimonies to piece together the puzzle surrounding these brutal murders. On going to the garage on his property, authorities encountered a foul-smelling drainage ditch. The smell was distinct, a smell that law enforcement associated with dead and decaying human remains. While many law enforcement officials were busy digging up human remains in the garage, others brought Powers in for questioning, determined to extract the truth from him. The interrogation was intense, with detectives grilling him about his motives and the gruesome details of the murders. Powers, however, remained defiant and initially refused to cooperate, cunningly evading their questions. The investigators knew they had to push harder, employing psychological tactics to break his resolve and make him confess to his heinous crimes, as well as hitting him with the hammer that he used to kill young Harry Eicher. After several hours of physical tactics (that Powers claimed as abuse), Harry F. Powers confessed to the murders of Dorothy Lemke, Asta Eicher and her three children.

THE TWENTY-SEVEN LETTERS
AND A WIDOW GONE MISSING

On Wednesday, August 26, 1931, law enforcement officials in Park Ridge, Illinois, contacted law enforcement in Clarksburg, West Virginia, about the disappearance of a widowed mother of three and her children who had been missing for well over two months. Her name was Asta Eicher, and twenty-seven letters had been sent to her from a Clarksburg, West Virginia address. The person of interest was a man by the name of Cornelius O. Pierson. Authorities in Clarksburg were not familiar with the name. A bit of investigation led Chief of Police C.A. Ducksworth, Sheriff of Harrison County W.B. Grimm, Deputy Sheriff H.H. Heught and Lead Detective Carl Southern to learn that a Cornelius O. Pierson had indeed rented box number 277 at the local post office. Further probing led Detective Southern to 111 Quincy Street in the Clarksburg suburb of Broad Oaks. It wasn't long before Detective Southern made the connection between the man of the house—a Mr. Harry Powers—and Cornelius O. Pierson.

Presides at bluebeard trial (The Judge). *West Virginia Archives.*

THE TAKEDOWN AND THE FIRST FORTY-EIGHT HOURS

It was a stakeout at the Powers home. He was not there, so the local police waited patiently for Powers to return. By high noon on August 27, 1931, he had arrived back to the home that he shared with his wife. Instead of being greeted by Luella, he was arrested on charges of manslaughter. The clank of handcuffs resonated in the air as officers shackled his wrists and declared him the prime suspect in the disappearance of the widow Eicher and her three children. In contemporary society, the charge might be dismissed due to lack of evidence; however, in 1931 suspicion was enough to detain a suspect. When Powers was arrested, he had five letters addressed to five different women across the country in his possession. Bingo! The police were on to something, and the investigation progressed rather quickly.

While at the Powers residence, the police on the scene learned about a farm near the property owned by the couple that had a newly erected garage. Strange. What on earth would a grocery store owner need with a garage on a farm that was not in the same location as the house? The garage was relatively small, so it would not have taken up much space. And yet it was an estimated mile and a half away from the home, in an area known

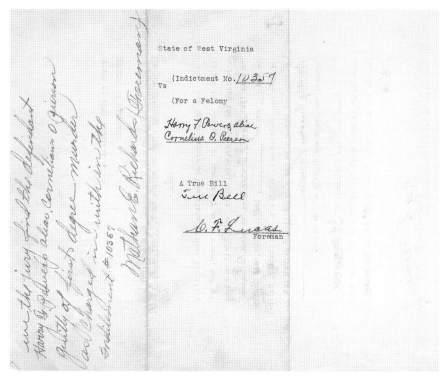

78

State of West Virginia,

        vs.   ///   Upon indictment for a felony.

Harry F. Powers, alias Cornelius O. Pierson.

INSTRUCTIONS ASKED FOR ON BEHALF OF THE DEFENDANT.

1.   The court instructs the jury that the indictment in
this case does not raise the slightest presumption of guilt
against the accused; but on the contrary the defendant is pre-
sumed to be innocent of the offense with which he is charged and
that presumption continues and remains with the accused throughout the trial and every stage thereof and until the state has
established by clear, distinct and reliable evidence and to the
exclusion of all reasonable doubt every element essential to
the crime charged against the accused; and failing in such proof,
or if upon completion of the testimony you, or any one of you
entertain any reasonable doubt as to the guilt of the defendant,
then, *you can not find the defendant guilty* ~~it is your duty to return a verdict of not guilty.~~

Opposite: Indictment of Harry F. Powers. *West Virginia Archives.*

Above: Court instructions to the jury. *West Virginia Archives.*

as Nutter's Fort. The farm provided a way to forcibly place the victims into captivity away from the prying eyes of neighbors. It was those very neighborly prying eyes that assisted in opening what came to be known as the murder garage. Initially, only dried blood was found, which was quite peculiar. An investigative mind would no doubt wonder whose blood it was, especially in light of the missing mother and children.

It was the morning of August 28, 1931, and with Powers in custody, law enforcement made their way down to the garage, where a trapdoor was found. On opening the door, they found jewelry and clothes were piled up, soaked in blood. With DNA testing nonexistent back then, the police had to rely on the testimony or possible confession from Powers. Blankly, he stared at the odd scene. The clothes clearly were not his, and the police asked him who they belonged to. Powers gave them absolutely nothing. Did he admit that the scene looked odd? Sure he did. He absolutely agreed with law enforcement that the clothes, jewelry and dried blood were a bit suspicious, but he never admitted to any wrongdoing, nor did he offer an explanation as to why there were blood-soaked clothes, jewelry and a noose hanging from the rafter of a secret room in the garage obscured by a trapdoor.

Powers played the role and dumbed himself down completely, feigning innocence, pretending not to know anything about the suspicious bloody artifacts in the garage or the mysterious disappearance of the widow Eicher and her children. While Powers continued to declare his innocence in police custody, a teenaged boy from Quiet Dell led police at the crime scene to a ditch alongside the garage. High noon was never a time, but always an event, and on Friday, August 28, 1931, in Clarksburg, at that very ditch, horror came at high noon as the bodies of the widow Eicher and her three children were found, decomposing, with their hands bound by what looked to be the same rope as the rope that was used to make the noose found in the rafter of the secret room in the garage.

The air was hot, thick and tense as the bodies of the Eicher family were removed from the ditch. It was obvious that they had been deceased for quite some time and the summer heat dd not do much in the way of slowing down the decomposition. While Asta and the two girls were strangled, Harry suffered a more heinous fate—he died from blunt force trauma to the head. It appeared that he had been struck with the hammer that was found at the crime scene. It would be a full forty-eight hours before the remains from the last victim, Dorothy Lemke, were found. Many reports at the time alleged that Lemke might have been the last to be killed by Powers; however, his confession told a more sinister tale. Word traveled quickly about the grisly findings of the Eicher family, and within twenty-four hours, thousands of people had arrived outside of the jail where Powers was detained. The mob grew angry and ready to take matters into their own hands if the authorities did not handle things appropriately.

THE INQUISITION AND THE "CHICAGO TUNE-UP"

The interrogation methods used by law enforcement in the 1930s were much different than today. Believe it or not, contemporary interrogation techniques are mild, more professional even. Bear in mind, it was at this time in America's history that crime—ergo criminal activity—was at its peak. The Great Depression ushered in a time of unimaginable insanity where people would commit heinous crimes and were uninhibited because people with nothing to lose are the most dangerous people of all. Baltasar Gracián and James Baldwin have left many quotes about people with nothing to lose.

Powers confessing to police. *West Virginia Archives.*

State of West Virginia
    vs. // Upon an Indictment for a Felony No. 10357
Harry F. Powers, alias Cornelius O. Pierson.

    This day came again the State by her Prosecuting Attorney as well as the defendant, Harry F. Powers, alias Cornelius O. Pierson, in person, who was set to the bar of the Court in the custody of the Sheriff and jailer of this County, and represented by J. E. Law, his attorney; and the motion of the defendant, made at a former day of this court, to set aside the verdict returned by the jury in this action on the 10th day of December, 1931, and to grant him a new trial herein having been argued by counsel and considered by the Court is hereby overruled and said new trial denied; to which ruling and action of the Court in overruling said motion and refusing a new trial herein the said defendant duly excepted.

    And it being demanded of the said defendant if there was anything he knew or had to say why the sentence of the Court should not be pronounced against him, and nothing being urged in delay thereof, it is considered and ordered by the Court that he, the said Harry F. Powers, alias Cornelius O. Pierson, be hung by the neck until he is dead, and the execution of this judgment to be done upon him, the said Harry F. Powers, alias Cornelius O. Pierson, by the Warden of the penitentiary of this State at Moundsville on Friday, the 18th day of March, in the year nineteen hundred and thirty-two; said execution to take place within the walls of said penitentiary according to law.

    The Clerk of this court is hereby directed to deliver a copy of this order to W. B. Grimm, Sheriff and jailer of this County, who shall retain the custody of the said Harry F. Powers, alias Cornelius O. Pierson, until a properly authorized guard, sent by the Warden of said penitentiary to receive him, shall convey said defendant, Harry F. Powers, alias Cornelius O. Pierson, to said penitentiary; and the Clerk shall also notify the

Warden of said penitentiary of the conviction and sentence of the
said defendant that he may as soon as practicable be removed and
safely conveyed to said institution there to be kept in the manner
provided by law until the said 18th day of March, 1932, when the
execution of the judgment aforesaid shall be done upon him, the
said Harry F. Powers, alias Cornelius O. Pierson.

And the said defendant expressing a desire to apply for
a writ of error and supersedeas to the judgment aforesaid, it is
ordered that the execution thereof be, and the same is hereby
suspended until the first day of the March Term, 1932 of this
court, to enable the said defendant to make such application.
and the said defendant hath leave to prepare, tender and have his
bill or bills of exception signed, sealed and made part of the
record herein within sixty (60) days from the adjournment of the
present term of court.

Thereupon the said defendant was remanded to jail in
the custody of the Sheriff and jailer of this County.

This page and opposite: Indictment of Harry F. Powers, pages 1–2. *West Virginia Archives.*

So while the FBI named gangsters and hustlers on the public enemies list, little-known hillside and small-town killers were wreaking havoc for state law enforcement teams across the country. Much like today, each police squad operated like its own mini militia, albeit back then perhaps each unit represented the ideals (mission, vision, values of the people, community and elected officials) of the state as a separate nation state, which translates to law enforcement handling interrogations with less tact, diplomacy, neutrality or empathy. Currently, many police organizations employ empathy-based interrogation (EBI) tactics, but prior to the use of EBI, police units were results-driven organizations that would get the "bad guy" by any means necessary. In the case of Powers, the interrogation employed violence, which resulted in gaining a confession, especially surprising out of an individual whose personality bordered on psychopathy like Powers.

As Detective Carl Southern and Chief Duckworth questioned Powers, it comes as no surprise that he incessantly proclaimed his innocence. Allegedly, after a few rounds of "questions" and a "Chicago Tune-up" from Deputy Sheriff Simeon C. Bond that involved the use of the very hammer that was used to kill young Harry Eicher, Powers was more amenable with his confession. According to the *Defendant's Bill of Exceptions* court record of the case, when Powers requested to speak with his attorney, the request was denied and the alleged beating continued. Powers's attorney J.E. Law mentioned that "he was beaten over the head, arms, shoulders, back, [chest], and legs with a rubber hose, [and] a metal chain and rope....He was [then] kicked on the legs, in the bowels, privates, in the face, hit one the body with fists....He was hit on the head with a hammer by Deputy Sheriff Simeon C. Bond and he was told that it was the same hammed he'd used to kill the male child with."[20]

After the interrogation, Powers told his lawyer that he was coerced into signing off on a confession and he was denied certain rights. He protested that this was America, a place where even the allegedly guilty are entitled to a fair trial. In 1930s America, one was not innocent until proven guilty— they were guilty until proven innocent, especially when charged with the murders of women and children. Not just any woman, Asta Eicher was a respected artisan whose name was firmly inscribed on silver wares (plates, tea sets, etc.) in Illinois. She wasn't just some unknown lonely heart; she was not only the widow of a well-known silversmith but also a silversmith herself, known in art circles as "Anna Eicher." Her handwrought sterling silver utensils and bowls are still being auctioned online today. Powers would undoubtedly hang for his crimes. Of course, a trial would take place, as that is what the accused is always guaranteed—a *fair* trial in front of a jury of his peers—and that is exactly what Powers received.

A Media Frenzy

The media hype that surrounded the trial was unbelievable. Journalists from far and wide settled on Quiet Dell in order to get the scoop on who this mass murderer was. It was the newspapers and movies that gave the weary and destitute something to look forward to—some type of excitement to help them escape from the day-to-day strife of life, unemployment and bread and soup lines. People were struggling to survive, yet somehow the news of a multi or mass murderer (the term *serial killer* was not coined until the 1970s by the Behavioral Science Unit of the FBI) ensnaring innocent women by placing lonely hearts ads made their lives seem better in comparison.

One thing about Americans is that we love a good story, and between the bank robbers and mob bandits, Harry Powers, the Bluebeard of West Virginia, was something incredible—after all how on earth could something so ghastly happen in the coal mining state? It was during this time that the coal mining industry came dangerously close to collapsing under the weight of the Great Depression and the problems that plagued many of the mining towns. Children with no shoes on their feet could be seen sitting on the sidewalks, and women sold eggs at the courthouse square just to make ends meet. This was also a time when people canned their own vegetables and meat and worked from dawn to dusk on the farms, in the fields or in the coal mines. After the daily hard work and toiling, people needed an escape. The larger-than-life crimes of people like Powers provided an escape into the world of a madman whose crimes headlined the local papers.

In the first forty-eight hours of Powers being detained, news of the case hit the front page of nearly every major newspaper across the continental United States. People, especially neighbors, were being interviewed and provided their accounts of the events and their perspectives of Harry Powers; his wife, Luella; their store; and the newly minted murder garage. While Powers was being interrogated, a person close to the case, Evan Alan Bartlett, began drafting his narrative and interpretation of the crime. In it, he declared Powers to be "a sadist due to his deliberate planning and execution of the torture and murders of his victims."[21] He further noted that "Powers killed the children for the thrill of killing."[22] Bartlett even went so far as to reach out to the notable (and often hailed as the founding father of American physical anthropology) anthropologist Dr. Aleš Hrdlička. Hrdlička's assessment of Powers included the following: "he had a lust to kill," which was not to be confused (or conflated) with insanity, but Powers had a "lust to kill for killing's sake," which was an "animalistic urge native to lower animals." Further, Hrdlička noted that Powers's lust to kill was "far more powerful than any lust for profit [because] the lust to kill comes first.... The lust for profit was incidental."[23]

Meanwhile, inside the interrogation room, officers asked Powers if he was familiar with the French bluebeard Henri D. Landru, who committed similar crimes nearly fifteen years prior. The police thought that Powers

Top: Powers walking out of trial in handcuffs. *West Virginia Archives.*

Bottom: The murder garage where the bodies of the victims were found. *West Virginia Archives.*

might have modeled his crimes after those committed by Landru. But Powers neither confirmed nor denied the assertion. The questioning lasted well into the early morning, until Powers finally admitted to the murders. In his confession, he stated that he killed all of the victims on the same day—Asta first, then Henry and Annabel, then Dorothy Lemke and Greta last. Of the murders, he made the assertion that each victim succumbed to being murdered quietly. He also claimed that he drove the Eicher family from Illinois to Fairmont, West Virginia, and left them there prior to driving back to Illinois to get Asta's money. There were some accounts from Asta's neighbors seeing him and even asking about the whereabouts of Asta and the children, to which he replied they were preparing to move to Europe.

It was during the confession that Powers mentioned leaving Illinois and driving to Northboro, Massachusetts, to pick up Dorothy Lemke and from there driving back to Fairmont, West Virginia, and then taking Lemke and the Eichers to his garage to kill them all on July 29, 1931. All of this was utterly impossible. To complete such a drive now would be unreasonable, let alone back then. Besides, the autopsy revealed that Asta and the children had nothing in their stomachs, which indicated that they were starved to weaken them and possibly tortured prior to being murdered. Part of Powers's confession was published in the *Clarksburg Gazette* on Sunday, August 30, 1931. This was the same day that the confession was given to the police. It read as follows:

> *My name is Harry F. Powers alias Cornelius Orvin Pison. I did in the month of July 1931 murder Mrs. Asta Eicher and her three children. I further state that my wife (Luella) and sister-in-law (Eva) knew nothing of the slayings and are innocent of anything in connection with those murders.*

Interesting. Powers did not bother to use his legal name, Harm Drenth, in this confession. And as for any possible involvement that Luella may have had, authorities were not entirely convinced of her innocence. They found it hard to believe that she had been married to him for a full four years and wasn't the least suspicious of his murderous activities. The lingering question was, How could she not know? When questioned, she merely indicated that she never asked her husband about anything. Whenever she saw him writing letters, she just assumed they were related to the work he did in sales and left it alone, because his work in sales required that he be away for weeks at a time. On his return, he would often bring her glamourous gifts, which no doubt diverted her attention from him. It still didn't add up. How was she oblivious to murders taking place on her land? How could a wife not see what her husband was up to? Surely, she must have suspected something. But Luella maintained the innocence of her and her sister. She *appeared* completely shocked at the actions of her husband. However, Luella had a track record of marrying murderers—her first husband had been convicted of murder too.

Once the interrogation was over and Powers was escorted back to jail, he confided in a minister, telling him that he was tortured and forced to confess to a crime that he did not commit. Further, he said that the real murderer was a man by the name of Carl Rogers. Sure, the police followed up on the allegation, but all roads (and evidence) led to Powers. The police began receiving accounts from numerous women who claimed to be his fiancée and others thought they were well on their way to the altar with the madman and they had the letters to prove it. As reports poured in from women, journalists managed to find Powers's father, Wilko Drenth, who went on record about his son always being in trouble with the law. By the time the trial started, the mob of onlookers had grown exponentially. They called for Powers to go to the gallows. As a result of the unruly crowd, law enforcement temporarily transported Powers to the prison in Moundsville, West Virginia. Due to the magnitude of the crowd and the eye-for-an-eye fervor in the air, a new space had to be scouted out for the trial. The courthouse was too small. So it was decided that the trial would be held at the opera house in Clarksburg, West Virginia. Once the trial was underway, Powers was transferred back to the Clarksburg jail.

It was indeed the trial of the year, and due to its sensational nature an estimated two hundred reporters from various parts of the country descended on Clarksburg to cover the trial. The intense media attention and the presence of so many reporters created a frenzied atmosphere outside the courthouse. Every detail of the trial was scrutinized and reported on, making it nearly impossible for Powers to escape public scrutiny. The constant media presence also put pressure on the jury to deliver a just verdict, knowing that their decision would be highly publicized and analyzed. Ultimately, the combination of Kemper's testimony, the motive presented by the prosecution and the intense media attention surrounding the trial all worked against Powers, leaving little hope for his defense. The media presence underscored the national interest in the case and the widespread shock at Powers's heinous crimes. The trial was one of the most publicized events of its time. News outlets from across the country sent reporters to cover every detail of the trial, resulting in extensive media coverage that captivated the nation.

The public's fascination with the case was fueled by the gruesome details of Powers's heinous crimes, which were extensively discussed and analyzed in newspapers and on television. This intense media attention put immense pressure on the jury, as they were well aware that their verdict would be met with intense scrutiny and could potentially shape the public's perception of the justice system. The jury members found themselves in a difficult position, torn between the weight of their civic duty and the weight of public opinion. They knew that their decision

Right: *Daily News*, December 31, 1931. *Newspapers.com.*

Below: Mrs. Luella Strothers Powers, wife of Bluebeard. *West Virginia Archives.*

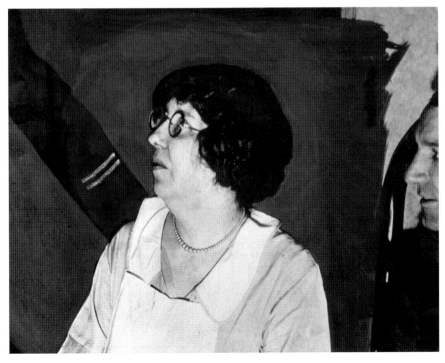

Daily News, December 11, 1931. *Newspapers.com.*

would not only determine Powers's fate but also have lasting implications on the public's trust in the justice system. Despite the pressure, the jury remained steadfast, carefully examining the evidence and deliberating for hours to ensure a fair and just verdict. Their commitment to upholding justice was commendable, as they understood the importance of their role in restoring public faith in the system. Their dedication to the task at hand was evident as they asked for clarification on certain points and reviewed the testimonies multiple times. The jury understood that their decision would have far-reaching consequences and that they had the power to either restore or further erode public trust in the justice system. In the end, their unanimous decision to convict Powers was a testament to their unwavering commitment to justice and their understanding of the weight of their responsibility. Their actions set a precedent for future juries, emphasizing the significance of their role in maintaining a fair and just society.

The trial, which began on December 7, 1931, was later relocated to an opera house that had 1,200 seats available for audience members. Despite the venue change, the furor surrounding Powers's case continued to escalate. The constant presence of a mob outside the opera house created a tense and intimidating environment for all involved. Security measures were heightened to ensure Powers's safety, with law enforcement officials working tirelessly to maintain order. The overwhelming public interest and the calls for the death penalty added an additional layer of complexity to an already challenging trial. The media frenzy surrounding Powers's case also reached a peak, with journalists camping outside the improvised courthouse day and night. With J. Edgar Hoover involved, the pressure for a swift and decisive verdict grew. Lawyers from both sides had to navigate the maze of public opinion, trying to ensure a fair trial free from external influence. The stakes were high, as the outcome of this trial would not only determine Powers's fate but also set a precedent for future cases involving violent crimes. Reporters dissected every piece of evidence and analyzed every witness statement, further fueling public interest. Politicians and activists continued to voice their opinions, putting even more pressure on the judges and jury to deliver a just verdict. The lawyers recognized the weight of their responsibility and worked tirelessly to present a comprehensive and compelling argument, knowing that the outcome would have far-reaching implications for the criminal justice system. The tension in the air was palpable as the trial unfolded, with both the prosecution and defense presenting their case with fervor and conviction.

"Bluebeard" Harry F. Powers at extreme left on trial in Clarksburg, West Virginia. *West Virginia Archives.*

Powers appeared unconcerned when the trial began, as evidenced by the fact that he chewed gum and yawned during the first day. The prosecution opened by reviewing the litany of stories told by Powers and how his account of traveling from West Virginia to Illinois then back to West Virginia and then over to Massachusetts made no sense. The prosecution further revealed how Powers strangled everyone except for Harry, whom he killed with a hammer. The horror of murdering women and children is a lot, and then to hear about one of the children being murdered with a hammer left the jury feeling mortified. After reading a letter that Powers wrote to his wife and sister-in-law, Eva, instructing them on how to prepare for and what to say if the police questioned them, the prosecution pretty much solidified their case against Powers. After all, why would an innocent man go through the trouble of warning his wife about law enforcement? An innocent would never resort to such behaviors.

During the trial, Powers still contended his innocence. He pointed the finger of blame on two mystery men—Cecil Johnson and Carl Rogers—neither of whom seemed to have anything to do with the crimes. As a matter of fact, when the authorities tracked down Rogers, he denied knowing Powers at all. Powers claimed that Johnson was a man whom Lemke was seen at a diner with prior to her untimely demise. None of the stories that he told made sense. He said that Rogers had a key to his garage where the bodies of the Eichers were found but could not attest to why. He explained that the suspicious bank transactions were related to his business dealings as a traveling salesman. When his attorney attempted to bring forth witnesses, none of them provided adequate testimony in support of his innocence. As the trial continued, Powers resorted to blaming the victims, stating that Lemke "abandoned him in Uniontown, Pennsylvania" when they were on their way to Clarksburg, West Virginia. He had also forged letters from the decedents as a means of creating an alibi.

By the time he was called to the witness stand, he was crying. He lied incessantly, blaming his wife for trapping him in a miserable marriage—even using this so-called misery as a reason why he had placed lonely hearts ads. As he told lie after lie, he didn't notice that he contradicted his earlier confession when he said under oath that the murders never occurred. This was all after law enforcement had collected evidence that suggested otherwise, revealing correspondence between Powers and several other women across the country who were convinced that they would marry him. Further, it was alleged that the police had in their possession notes indicating that he would have murdered his wife, Luella, had he not gotten caught.

The verdict was painfully obvious, so much so that when Powers's attorney gave his closing arguments, he too was crying and begging the jury to have mercy on his client. Mercy was highly unlikely given the magnitude of the crimes and the fact that Powers was toying with the court, pretending to be a wrongfully accused innocent man. The sordid details of the case had made their way to the front pages of nearly all of the mainstream newspapers. The horrible crime even inspired a song that recounted the events. While everyone anxiously awaited a decision from the jury, outside the opera house, a mob of citizens demanded justice for the victims and called for Powers to be executed. After the deliberation, the jury returned with a guilty verdict, which landed Powers on death row at the West Virginia Penitentiary in Moundsville, where he would be executed by hanging at the gallows. To be sentenced to death in 1931 meant that the execution would be carried out quickly. Prisoners were not living on death row for years (like many are today) after they were sentenced. If anything, the death sentence resulted in a quick execution date. For Powers, that date was March 18, 1932, at 9:00 a.m. Eastern Standard Time. Unfortunately, the sentence was not groundbreaking, as it has been alleged that Powers was the last person to be sentenced to death by hanging in the state of West Virginia.

```
STATE OF WEST VIRGINIA            )
                                  (        TO-WIT:
COUNTY OF HARRISON                )


    IN THE CRIMINAL COURT OF SAID COUNTY, November TERM,
                    1931.

        The Grand Jurors of the State of West Virginia,
    in and for the body of the County of Harrison, and now
    attending the said Criminal Court, upon their oaths
    present that Harry F. Powers, alias Cornelius O. Pierson,
    on the ___ day of _____, 1931, in the said County
    of Harrison, feloniously, willfully, maliciously, delib-
    erately and unlawfully did slay, kill and murder one
    Dorothy Pressler Lemke                             ,
    against the peace and dignity of the State.

        Found upon the testimony of C.A. Duckworth,
    duly sworn in open court to testify the truth and sent
    before the Grand Jury, this the 10th day of November,
    1931.

                            Will E. Morris
                            Prosecuting Attorney.
```

Prosecuting Attorney Declaration of Crime (Official Court Document). *West Virginia Archives.*

THE EXECUTION AT WEST VIRGINIA PENITENTIARY IN MOUNDSVILLE

The West Virginia State Penitentiary was undeniably one of the most deplorable correctional facilities operating at the time. The penitentiary is located in Moundsville, West Virginia, and is situated on land directly across from a Native American burial mound known as Grave Creek Mound that is approximately two thousand years old. The circumference of the mound is 240 feet, and it has a height of 62 feet, making it a conical burial cemetery. The ominous-looking Gothic edifice of the penitentiary dates back to its establishment in the year 1867. Even the most courageous individuals feel a chill down their backs when they encounter the spine-chilling atmosphere caused by the tall stone walls and dark, tiny windows of this structure. Walking through its massive gates gives the impression of going back in time; it's almost as though the ghosts of long-dead inmates are still lingering within the prison's walls. Those who have passed through the jail have been undoubtedly left with a profound impression courtesy of its intimidating appearance. The eerie silence that pervades the air only adds to the haunting allure of this prison. The sound of footsteps echoing through the cold corridors creates a sense of apprehension, as if the building itself is alive with the memories of past suffering. The stories of brutal punishments and desperate escape attempts only reinforce the prison's fearsome reputation. Even the most hardened souls cannot help but be affected by the oppressive atmosphere and the lingering presence of those who once called this place home. The dim flickering lights cast eerie shadows on the decaying walls, making it impossible to ignore the palpable sense of foreboding that hangs heavy in the air. Each creaking door and rustling of chains sends shivers down the spines of those who have ventured inside. It is said that the spirits of the tormented still wander these halls, their anguished cries echoing through the night.

On the day of the execution, a myriad of emotions shrouded the West Virginia Penitentiary. People from the community and members of the media were present, wondering if the condemned would feel fear, trepidation and most of all pain like that he inflicted on his victims. It is possible that execution at the gallows would result in a quick and painless death, but this would be contingent on the height of the drop. Powers ascended the thirteen steps leading to the gallows slow, steady and without emotion. The number thirteen was symbolic of the twelve individuals who comprised the jury and the one judge who presided over the case. When he was given the opportunity

POWERS FOUND GUILTY, MUST DIE ON GALLOWS

Police Hunt Rich Bride, 15, And Husband

FIFTEEN-YEAR-OLD Beatrice Barclay Pickerell, Montclair, N. J., heiress, vanished again yesterday, taking her truckman husband with her. The harried newlyweds took to flight a few leaps ahead of police, who sought to arrest the bridegroom on statutory charges.

In a vintage flivver, with only a few dollars between them, they set forth at the crack of dawn from the sanctuary at Essex Fells, N. J., where the schoolgirl bride had been living since she escaped from paternal captivity early Tuesday.

By nightfall police of half a dozen communities, augmented by details of State troopers, were patrolling a wide area seeking to head them off and wrest the girl from the arms of her spouse from whom she previously had been "kidnaped" by her parents.

Father Signs Charges.

The charges against Bevis T. Pickerell, the vanished bridegroom, were sworn to yesterday by the

Mrs. Beatrice Barclay Pickerell in dancing costume.

girl's father, John C. Barclay, a former vice-president of the Western Union Telegraph Company.

Barclay, who, with his son, Robert, a Lafayette College student, interrupted the girl's honeymoon, charged his unwelcome son-in-law with betraying his daughter and added an even, more serious accusation.

Although warrants were issued and police sought to serve them, there was considerable legal speculation as to whether they could be made to stand up in court. It was reported the irate parent also contemplated charging Pickerell with violation of the Mann act.

Warned, Couple Flees.

The 29-year-old bridegroom, after eloping with the schoolgirl from her New Jersey home, took

(Continued on page 8, col. 2)

Doomed Bluebeard, Victims, Accusers

Harry F. Powers, found guilty of first degree murder yesterday, as he appeared outside court with hands chained and manacled.

Mrs. Asta Eicher and her children—Harry, Greta and Annabelle—for whose murder Powers also stands accused.

Chief of Police Duckworth; Mrs. Charles Flemming, sister of victim and her husband.

Mrs. Dorothy Lemke, Powers' mail order sweetheart, for whose murder he was convicted yesterday by West Virginia jury.

State Scores Bluebeard As 'Arch Beast'

By JOHN O'DONNELL.
(Staff Correspondent)

CLARKSBURG, W. Va., Dec. 10.—Harry F. Powers, mass murderer of Quiet Dell, late this afternoon heard a jury announce he must die on the gallows for the murder of Mrs. Dorothy Pressler Lemke—one of the five victims strangled by the plump Romeo of the matrimonial agencies.

Stolidly, the man, who a few hours earlier heard himself denounced as a "beast, guilty of a crime of the ages," listened to the verdict without an expression on his face. For an hour and fifty minutes the jurors had debated his fate and the guilt of Powers had risen obviously as the minutes passed.

Believed He'd Get Life.

Like many among the 1,200 spectators who crammed the Moore Opera House, he believed the eloquence of his counsel, Attorney J. Ed. Law—who borrowed the idea of clemency—might bring a recommendation for life imprisonment.

There was not the slightest outbreak in the theatre when the verdict was announced. Deputy sheriffs, local police and State troopers lined the aisles on the orders of Judge John C. Southern to suppress the first outburst. There was none.

When the jury emerged to the stage from the star's dressing room where they conducted their deliberations, Powers glanced quickly at the first face, apparently read his fate and then turned away to whisper to his counsel.

"The jury has a verdict," Sheriff William Grimm declared formally to the judge.

Guilty in First Degree.

Judge Southern nodded to the clerk who took a paper held out

(Continued on page 4, col. 2)

Your Christmas List? Remember To Include This

By SALLY JOY BROWN.

How do you do, Good Fellows! Have you begun your Christmas shopping? Have you started the seemingly endless round of store to store admiring this, buying that? Have you begun checking off names from the list of people to whom you simply must give? Are you whispering about the big surprise in store for Jimmy, Mary and little Joe? Are you satisfied with what you're doing in everyone's behalf?

Wait a minute! Haven't you forgotten something?

Remember These?

What about that sad-faced woman you passed on your way to the shopping district? What about that weary-eyed man who asked you for a job? What about that family you read of in the papers where the parents, poor and disillusioned, killed themselves and left four youngsters to the mercy of strangers?

You shudder when you think of them, don't you? You say, perhaps, "I would love to do something big for the poor things, but I don't see how I can." You refuse to believe that there is tragedy right around the corner and go ahead with your plans for a happy Christmas in your own family.

Stop for a moment. There is a way in which you can help your unfortunate brothers and sisters. There is a means by which you can

(Continued on page 20)

3 Boys Held in Fatal Shooting of Woman

SCHOOLBOYS, holding nocturnal target practice from an attic window, fired the fusillade of bullets that pierced homes in West Orange, N. J., Wednesday night, and killed Mrs. Grace Giuliano, wife of a wealthy furrier, as she was about to step into her bath.

Erwin Flaster, 16, admitted to West Orange police last night that he fired the bullet which is believed to have ended Mrs. Giuliano's life. The boys were in the attic of the Flaster home at 139 Gregory Ave., a block behind the Giuliano house at 5 Colony Drive West.

Shooting at Lights.

"We were shooting at lights and telephone wires with the gun I bought at camp last summer," the Flaster boy confessed after detectives had taken him into custody at West Orange High School.

"We had fired ten or twelve times. It was my turn and I aimed at a light on a telephone pole. Right after I fired we heard a woman scream, so we didn't shoot any more."

Taken from the high school classroom with the Flaster boy was William Fieldman, 14, of 47 Colony Drive East, who admitted he was one of the group in the attic.

Edwin Schaller, 16, of 28 Cobane Terrace, confessed to being the third marksman. After the screams were heard, he said, he took the rifle home with him to clean it.

Fourth Boy Denies Guilt.

Robert Blair, 18, of 77 Corbane Place, admitted to police that he was with the boy Sunday night when they fired at targets from the Flaster attic, but denied that he was present Wednesday night.

The boys said they practiced on numerous occasions with Flaster's gun.

Mrs. Giuliano, daughter of John Moffatt, labor conciliator of the

(Continued on page 4, col. 1)

The West Orange, N. J., home in which Mrs. Grace Giuliano was shot to death.

HUNT HIT-RUNNER WHO HURT WOMAN

Police searched yesterday for the driver of an auto which knocked down and ran over Mrs. Marguerite Gibson, 27, and Mrs. Mary Mooney, 27, both of 741 East Third St., Brooklyn, Wednesday night, as the two women crossed 18th Ave., Brooklyn. Both victims were taken to United Israel Hospital. Their injuries are serious.

(Picture on page 1)

Broiled fresh **mushrooms**

an award-nutritional. Grilled in butter, broiled on toast, baked, fried. Gives the family a treat. Mushrooms are now at prices down so you can reach. And everyone likes mushrooms either in a national occasion it has both tender such requisite strength and be.

DICK TRACY

Vigilante, star sleuth, gangster enemy. He rattles the racketeer, "gets" the gangster! Follow his thrill-filled career every day and now—Sunday—

in full color pages starting in next Sunday's

SUNDAY NEWS
New York's Picture Newspaper

to utter a few final words as a noose consisting of thirteen loops was placed over his head, he opted only to say one word prior to being put to death: "No." As the trapdoor opened, almost instantly, his body fell, and the rope jerked taut around his neck, causing him to be strangled. The dislocation of his neck bone and severing of his spinal cord resulted in near-instant death and marked the end of the life of this most heinous killer. As his lifeless body swung gently back and forth, a grim reminder of the monstrous acts he had committed, the executioner stepped forward to confirm that justice had been served, checking for any signs of life. Satisfied that the man was truly gone, he signaled for the body to be taken down and prepared for burial. The town breathed a collective sigh of relief, finally able to move forward from the terror that had plagued the citizens for far too long.

While the execution brought a sense of catharsis to many, it also sparked protests and demonstrations. Some activists, citing concerns over the ethics of capital punishment, called for a reevaluation of the justice system. Meanwhile, the families and friends of the victims found solace in the knowledge that Powers's reign of terror had finally come to an end. The execution of Harry F. Powers left an indelible mark on both the community of Quiet Dell and the state of West Virginia at-large. Shocked by the extent of his crimes, society began questioning the prevailing attitudes toward crime and punishment. The case served as a catalyst for legal reforms, illuminating the need for stricter regulations regarding personal ads and fostering a collective determination to prevent similar tragedies in the future.

The chilling saga of Harry F. Powers will forever be etched in the history of Quiet Dell. It serves as a cautionary tale, reminding society of the darkness that can lurk behind seemingly ordinary faces. The community healed, and it is our duty to reflect on the execution's wider ramifications, sparing no effort in creating a society that safeguards its most vulnerable members, as well as ensuring that justice is swift and certain for those who seek to prey on them.

A Twist of Irony

After the conviction and execution of Powers, it seemed that justice was served for his victims. But nearly a year later, in 1933, his father, seventy-one-year-old Wilko Drenth, died by suicide in a most horrendous way.

He had been living in an Iowa village in LeRoy Township at the home of his daughter and son-in-law, Everett Schroeder, amid other Dutch locals. According to the Thursday, October 12, 1933 edition of the *Sumner Gazette*, Wilko used a ".38 caliber shotgun, and shot himself in the chest." Apparently, Wilko had been living there for four years, and on the previous Friday afternoon (October 6), he decided to end his life. Sadly, his grandson discovered his remains when he came home from working in the field around 3:15 p.m. The clothes that surrounded the entry wound of his chest were said to be smoldering from the point-blank range from which Wilko had shot himself. The article went on to state that Wilko had been in good health and in a good mood prior to the suicide. Further, he and his son-in-law had planned on visiting Michigan within the following month. It added that Wilko had been a widower for nearly five years, four of which he had lived with his daughter, son-in-law and grandchildren. Finally, the article notes that Wilko's family did not believe that his suicide had anything to do with the murderous actions of Harry Powers. The irony here is that Wilko probably killed himself because of the shame that Powers brought on the family name. He came to America as an immigrant, seeking to provide a new and positive life for his family. While Wilko may have been estranged from Powers (his third and middle child), it still does not eradicate the fact that his own son—his flesh and blood—committed such atrocities. As an immigrant, he brought with him values that he shared with his ethnic community group. The actions committed by Harry were utterly dishonorable and went against the values that those within Wilko's ethnic community shared. It could be highly likely that the phrase "death before dishonor" resonated within Wilko's community group, or it is possible Wilko felt that his suicide could possibly restore honor to the family name.

The shame and disgrace brought on Wilko's family by Harry's actions may have been unbearable for him. He might have believed that taking his own life was the only way to cleanse the family name and restore their honor in the eyes of their community. The weight of shame and guilt must have been unbearable for Wilko, knowing that his own son had brought disgrace down on their family. As a member of his ethnic community, Wilko understood the importance of upholding moral values and maintaining honor. It is conceivable that Wilko saw suicide as a desperate attempt to redeem the family's reputation and restore honor, even if it meant sacrificing his own life. The pain of seeing his son's dishonorable actions may have driven him to believe that death was the only way to find solace and regain a sense of dignity. While it is possible that Wilko's suicide was driven by a desire to restore honor to his family name, it is also important to consider other factors such as mental health issues or personal struggles that may have contributed to his decision.

The weight of societal expectations and the fear of judgment from his community may have further fueled Wilko's belief that suicide was the ultimate solution. In his mind, ending his own life might have been seen as a noble act, a way to atone for his son's wrongdoing and protect the family's legacy. Tragically, Wilko's desperation to restore honor overshadowed his ability to seek alternative means of redemption or support, ultimately leading to a devastating and irreversible decision. Wilko's internal struggle was undoubtedly amplified by the cultural norms and values deeply ingrained within his community. The pressure to conform to societal expectations and maintain a pristine reputation can be overwhelming, especially in tight-knit communities where reputation is everything. The fear of judgment and the potential loss of respect from his peers and loved ones may have driven Wilko to believe that suicide was the only path to redemption. In his mind, sacrificing his own life was a way to cleanse the family name and preserve their honor. However, this tragic perspective prevented him from seeing the countless alternative paths toward healing and finding support.

5

THE DENOUEMENT

The trial of Harry F. Powers captivated the nation as details of his heinous crimes were disclosed during court proceedings. At the time, his case shook the foundations of society and served as an example of how evil can conceal itself beneath an alluring exterior. It serves as a disturbing reminder that monsters can exist even among those of us who appear to be normal. True manipulator that he was, Powers delighted in luring his victims to his West Virginia property under false pretenses before committing heinous acts of violence against them. The deliberate and calculated nature of his crimes, coupled with the long-lasting emotional, psychological and physical wounds inflicted on his victims, demonstrates that Powers's sadistic tendencies cannot be attributed solely to mental health or external factors. The accounts of the victims' trauma and suffering prior to their murders served as a stark reminder of the enduring consequences of Powers's actions. The bravery of the dozens of women who had contact with Powers to come forward and share their stories not only revealed the extent of his calculating nature but also served as a catalyst for justice. It was essential that the court recognize the experiences of these women and hold Powers accountable for the irreparable harm he caused. The collective response to this case served as a wake-up call to prioritize the safety and well-being of vulnerable individuals within the community and the nation at large in order to ensure that no one else fell victim to such sadistic acts. Harry F. Powers's legacy serves as a haunting reminder of the depths to which human depravity can sink.

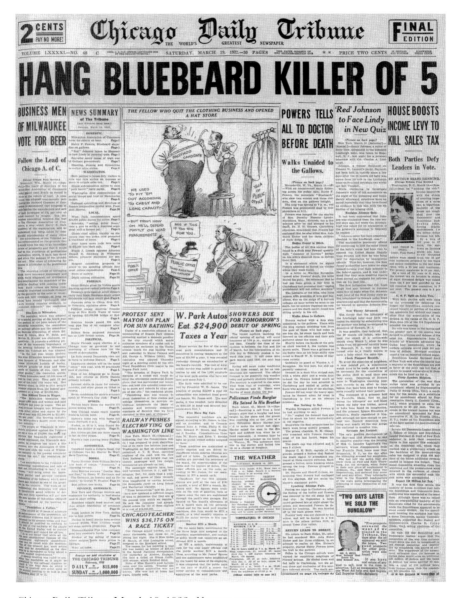

Chicago Daily Tribune, March 19, 1932. *Newspapers.com.*

The Birth of the American Serial Killer

Powers's crimes have since become commonplace among contemporary serial murderers, which is an intriguing fact. Since his execution, there have been no imitators of his offenses, but there was a serial killer with an uncannily similar modus operandi. He was identified as John Edward Robinson. Powers and Robinson share a disturbing similarity in their exceptional ability to manipulate their victims. Powers preyed on vulnerable widows and divorcées by placing personal ads in newspapers, promising them affection, security and financial stability. Robinson used online advertisements to exploit the desires and delusions of women interested in BDSM. Both men created false identities to exploit their victims' vulnerabilities and insecurities, enticing them into their web of deceit and control. For instance, throughout his illicit career, Powers assumed various aliases in order to deceive and avoid suspicion. Similarly, Robinson concealed his true identity behind a plethora of online personas, using the anonymity afforded by the internet to trap his victims.

This shared manipulative technique is significant because it establishes a correlation between the perpetrators' psychological strategies. It highlights the calculated and predatory nature of their offenses, as they exploited the victims' emotional desire for companionship and adventure. By analyzing this similarity, we gain insight into the psychological landscape of serial killers, revealing the common techniques they employ to obtain the trust of their victims. The second remarkable similarity between Powers and Robinson is their use of deception to gain proximity to their victims. Powers meticulously cultivated trust through a blend of charisma, assurances of love and safety and captivating storytelling. Robinson, who was skilled at creating the illusion of credibility, used online personas and fabricated stories to win his victims' trust. Both criminals exploited the societal belief in the kindness of others, preying on the vulnerability of their victims and exploiting their yearning for genuine connections.

This similarity has profound ramifications, as it reveals the grim reality that predators like Powers and Robinson can thrive by exploiting the fundamental human virtues of trust and compassion. This parallel provides a deeper comprehension of the depths to which individuals can sink when motivated by sinister intentions. Powers and Robinson share a third significant similarity in their ability to conceal their illicit activities. Aware of the suspicions of law enforcement, Powers carried out his heinous deeds with the utmost care, ensuring that no traces were left behind. Robinson, with his knowledge of the internet's anonymity and encryption, employed elaborate strategies and complex layers of deceit, leaving few traces of his criminal activity. Both individuals exhibited a high degree of cunning and strategic planning to avoid detection, exercising control over their environments. This shared ability to conceal their offenses allowed Powers and Robinson to evade suspicion for extended periods, compounding the suffering of their victims. By deciphering this similarity, valuable insights into the dark psyche of serial killers are obtained, namely how their cunning and meticulous actions contribute to their evasive nature. In addition to their murderous actions, both Powers and Robinson committed fraud and extortion. Both individuals were motivated by a desire for financial gain as well as power.

Examining the notorious criminals Harry F. Powers and John Edward Robinson reveals incontrovertible parallels between their methods and motivations. Both individuals' manipulative strategies, exploitation of trust and concealment of criminal activities provide chilling insight into the psychopathology of serial murderers.

As society continues to contend with the eerie legacies of Powers and Robinson, it is vital to remain vigilant and aware of the warning signs that criminals inspired by their actions may exhibit. Through continued research, public education and effective law enforcement, we can protect the vulnerable and prevent the emergence of future perpetrators who may seek to replicate the depravity and destruction inflicted by Powers and Robinson. The similarities between these criminals serve as a sobering reminder of the need for continual vigilance, unwavering dedication to justice and compassion.

THE CONTINUING INFLUENCE OF HARRY F. POWERS'S CRIMES ON THE TRUE CRIME GENRE

The extensive documentation of Harry F. Powers' chilling crimes in true crime literature provides a deep insight into the twisted psyche of the culprit and the dark consequences that followed. As a matter of fact, two fiction books (*Quiet Dell* by Jayne Anne Phillips and *The Night of the Hunter* by Davis Grubb), two nonfiction books (*The Mail Order Serial Killer: The Life and Death of Harry Powers* by Dr. Vance McLaughlin and *Love Murders of Harry F. Powers: Beware Such Bluebeards* by Evan Allan Bartlett), a crime file series chapbook (*The Bluebeard of West Virginia: The Infamous Quiet Dell Murders* by Douglas MacGowan), a film (*Night of the Hunter* by Charles Laughton) and a documentary (*Romeo Must Hang* by Robert Tinnell and Bob Wilkinson) on his horrible crimes were published. Renowned authors, such as Ann Rule and Truman Capote, have skillfully delved into these events, recounting the crimes with a personal touch. For example, Ann Rule's seminal work *The Stranger Beside Me* (2004) draws on her own experiences and relationship with a killer to present a harrowing account. Similarly, Truman Capote's groundbreaking book *In Cold Blood* (1966) meticulously reconstructs the events surrounding brutal murders, capturing the attention and horror of readers. These literary works showcase the psychological depths of the criminal mind through various compelling techniques, including vivid descriptions, suspenseful storytelling and comprehensive character analysis. By examining Powers's crimes in true crime literature, authors not only shed light on his sinister actions but also contribute to the development and evolution of the genre itself.

The Legacy of Powers's Crimes in Contemporary Society

Harry F. Powers is indeed one of the forefathers of the American serial killer. His crimes have shaped the true crime genre, influencing its trajectory and ensuring its continued relevance in contemporary society. The profound effect of Powers's manipulation tactics, luring techniques and the subsequent investigation and capture have left an indelible mark on storytelling techniques employed in true crime literature, films and documentaries. The enduring public fascination with the darkest corners of humanity, as exemplified by Powers's crimes, continues to fuel the demand for true crime media, propelling the genre forward. Furthermore, the examination and analysis of the profound consequences of Powers's crimes not only provide riveting entertainment but also contribute to the collective understanding of crime and its implications for society. Powers's crimes serve as a cautionary tale, reminding us of the depths of depravity that humans are capable of and encouraging ongoing discussions on trust, manipulation and the pursuit of justice in a world that is endlessly intrigued by stories of true crime.

The deeds of Harry Powers and the mythological legend of Bluebeard are both still relevant in modern times. The Bluebeard of Quiet Dell gained notoriety for his heinous deeds, which included luring helpless women with lonely hearts adverts and then murdering them together with their children. His crimes earned him the bluebeard moniker. During the 1930s, his acts caused shockwaves to travel across the country, and the general public wanted swift revenge. The case of Harry Powers, also known as the "Lonely Hearts Killer," continues to captivate the public's imagination due to its chilling similarities to modern cases of online dating scams and serial killers who prey on vulnerable individuals. The Bluebeard legend, symbolizing the dark depths of human nature and the predatory nature of men, still resonates in society as a cautionary tale against falling for charismatic but dangerous individuals. Although the methods and motives may have evolved, the enduring relevance of these stories underscores the timeless fascination with the darkness that lurks within human hearts. These cautionary tales remind us that while technology may have changed the way we connect with others, the dangers of trusting strangers remain the same. In today's digital age, online dating scams exploit the vulnerability of individuals searching for love, often leading to financial ruin and emotional devastation. Similarly, modern serial killers who prey on the vulnerable demonstrate that the darkness within human hearts still exists, creating a terrifying parallel to the long-standing Bluebeard legend of the monstrous husband who murdered his wives. Just as Bluebeard lured his victims with charm and deceit, these contemporary killers use social media platforms and dating apps to gain the trust of their unsuspecting targets. The chilling reality is that while technology has evolved, the darkness that drives individuals to commit such heinous acts remains a haunting reminder of the depths of human depravity. These modern-day predators exploit the anonymity and perceived safety of online interactions, allowing them to manipulate their victims with ease. They carefully craft their online personas, presenting themselves as charming, kindhearted individuals while hiding their true intentions. The alarming frequency of such incidents serves as a stark reminder that despite all the progress we have made as a society, the capacity for evil still lurks within the human soul. These are cautionary tales that reveal a sad reality: despite the advancements in technology, the essence of human nature remains unchanged.

The cautionary tales of Bluebeard and the modern-day dangers of online dating scams and serial killers highlight the need for vigilance and awareness when it comes to trusting others, whether in the physical or digital realm. It is a chilling realization that the darkness within human hearts continues to manifest itself in different forms, reminding us that the age-old lessons of caution and skepticism are as relevant today as they were centuries ago. In a world that is becoming increasingly interconnected, the potential for deception and manipulation has only grown. The rise of social media platforms and online communities has provided a breeding ground for individuals with malicious intentions, making it imperative for individuals to exercise caution and discernment. However, amid the disheartening reality, there is also hope. The same technological advancements that have given rise to these dangers can also empower individuals to educate themselves, share stories and collectively work toward creating a safer and more trusting society. By using these platforms responsibly, individuals can raise awareness about online threats, promote digital literacy and foster a sense of community that actively supports one another. Moreover, law enforcement agencies and tech companies are increasingly implementing measures to combat online harassment and protect user privacy. With continued efforts and collaborative initiatives, there is a possibility of harnessing technology's potential for positive change, ultimately creating an internet environment that is both safe and inclusive for all.

In recent years, there has been a growing recognition of the importance of addressing online threats and promoting digital literacy. Many organizations and individuals have taken it upon themselves to raise awareness about the various forms of online harassment and educate people on how to protect themselves. This collective effort is crucial in creating a safer online space for everyone. Additionally, law enforcement agencies and tech companies have also stepped up their efforts to combat online harassment and protect user privacy. They have implemented various measures such as stricter regulations, advanced security features and improved reporting systems to address these issues. This collaborative approach between different stakeholders is essential in effectively addressing the ever-evolving nature of online harassment. By working together, individuals, law enforcement agencies and tech companies can stay one step ahead of cybercriminals. Educating users about online safety, promoting responsible online behavior and continually updating security measures will help maintain a safer digital environment for all. With increased awareness and proactive measures, we can create a cyberspace where individuals can freely express themselves without fear of harassment or privacy breaches. Additionally, establishing clear and enforceable laws against online harassment will serve as a deterrent and provide victims with legal recourse. Collaboration between different stakeholders is crucial in developing effective strategies to combat cyberbullying, cyberstalking and other forms of online harassment. By fostering a culture of respect and empathy online, we can cultivate a more inclusive and supportive digital community. Ultimately, it is our collective responsibility to safeguard the digital space and protect the rights and well-being of all individuals.

POWERS'S LASTING INFLUENCE ON A NEW GENERATION OF CRIMINALS

A chilling legacy persists in the annals of criminal history, as the crimes of Harry F. Powers continue to resonate in the actions of a new generation of serial killers. In a dark era marked by vulnerability and manipulation, Powers emerged as a master of deceit, leaving a trail of devastation in his wake. His heinous acts have not only scarred the past but have also spawned a disturbing resurgence of predators targeting vulnerable women and children. Powers, also known as the "Bluebeard of Quiet Dell," operated during the 1930s, ensnaring his victims using personal ads. Drawing inspiration from a centuries-old European fairy tale that tells the story of a wealthy man who murders his wives, Powers adapted the narrative to his own terrifying reality. His charming and charismatic façade masked a sinister motive, luring innocent women into a web of deceit that ultimately led to their demise. Through manipulation and calculated brutality, Powers extinguished the lives of these unsuspecting individuals, forever altering the course of their families' destinies. He meticulously planned his crimes, gaining the trust of his victims by weaving elaborate tales of love and security. Yet behind closed doors, he transformed into a sadistic murderer, inflicting unimaginable pain and suffering on those who had fallen into his trap.

The media frenzy surrounding Powers's case was unprecedented in its intensity. Newspapers eagerly painted vivid portraits of his crimes, capturing the macabre imagination of a nation gripped by fear. The public was captivated by the audacity and cruelty of his actions, unable to comprehend how such evil could exist in their midst. But Powers's influence did not die with him. In recent years, a disturbing trend has emerged: a new generation of serial killers seemingly inspired by the malevolence of Powers. These contemporary criminals share striking similarities in their methods and motives, targeting vulnerable women and children with calculated precision. Research and investigations into these modern-day predators have revealed a haunting parallel between Powers and their actions. From their use of personal ads to establish relationships with victims to their ability to manipulate and exploit insecurities, these killers echo Powers's sinister tactics. Like him, they seek out the vulnerable and prey on their trust, using charm and deception to mask their true intentions.

When examining their modus operandi, the resemblance to the blueprint laid out by the original master of deception becomes clear. Just as Powers meticulously planned his crimes, these contemporary killers leave no detail to chance. They carefully select their victims, groom them and gradually erode their defenses, building a connection that eventually allows them to strike. Their methods reflect a deep understanding of the vulnerabilities and desires that Powers mercilessly exploited. Experts, in their attempts to understand and decipher the minds of these contemporary killers, have turned to Powers as a reference point. Psychological analysis has revealed an unsettling thread connecting Powers's crimes to the twisted motivations of his successors. It appears that his reign of terror exerted an enduring influence, igniting a twisted fascination within individuals seeking to replicate his heinous acts.

The implications of this influence are far-reaching. Law enforcement agencies have faced increasing challenges in detecting and apprehending these criminals as they adopt the methods perfected by Powers. The intricacy of their deceptions, honed by Powers's example, frustrates investigative efforts and prolongs their reigns of terror. Consequently, a renewed emphasis on profiling techniques and preventative measures has emerged, born out of the need to understand and combat the influence of Powers and his disciples. Experts meticulously study the patterns, techniques and psychological makeup of both Powers and the modern-day serial killers, hoping to identify key characteristics that can aid in their detection and prevention. The goal is to dismantle the twisted legacy he left behind, but progress is painstakingly slow. The toll on the families and communities affected by these crimes remains immeasurable, forever scarred by the haunting specter of Powers and his malevolent successors. The legacy of these crimes extends beyond the immediate victims; it leaves scars on the collective psyche of society, forever changing the way we view vulnerability and trust. As readers grapple with the chilling reality of Powers's influence, it becomes imperative to acknowledge the lasting effect of historical serial killers on current crime trends. Only by studying their methods, motives and psychological profiles can we hope to prevent future generations of criminals from succumbing to this dark allure. It is a somber reminder that the fight against evil is ongoing, requiring vigilance, empathy and unity to protect our most vulnerable members of society.

When researching the criminal career of Harry F. Powers, I noticed that there were many striking similarities between him and Henri Désiré Landru. It was easy to see why the police on the Powers case made the connection between him and Landru and why they may have even thought, if only for an instant, that he was a copycat killer. Back in the 1930s, this nomenclature might not have been used, but the Powers case file revealed that law enforcement noticed the similarities between the two killers. Powers and Landru were architects of terror, weaving webs of manipulation, deceit and cold-blooded violence that engulfed their victims in a macabre dance of fear. Indeed, fear is a dance that can only end when faith steps in, and unfortunately the victims were ensnared in the terror that those two murderers propagated. Drawing parallels between Powers and Landru, unfurling the intricate tapestry of their criminal methods, delving into their personalities, motivations, profiles, victim typologies and their dogged determination to evade capture are things that might be able to help people better understand these types of predators. Moreover, it will aid in the prevention of people becoming victims to them.

Both Powers and Landru employed similar criminal methods, such as using deception to lure their victims and manipulating their emotions to gain their trust. To gain the confidence of their targets, they presented themselves as trustworthy individuals, relying on charm and charisma. By assuming the guise of respectable and reliable figures, they disarmed their victims, creating a false sense of security. Deception played a pivotal role in Powers's and Landru's crimes, allowing them to manipulate their victims into more vulnerable situations that would lead to the inevitable. This tactic not only established control over their victims but also enabled the execution of their heinous acts without raising suspicion. In addition to deception, Powers and Landru employed manipulative tactics and showcased psychological traits that allowed them to earn their victims' trust. They demonstrated exceptional skill in identifying and exploiting the vulnerabilities of their victims, carefully tailoring their approach based on individual needs and desires.

Both Powers and Landru excelled at creating emotional connections, presenting themselves as empathetic and understanding individuals. Their manipulative tactics included showing feigned interest, sympathy and compassion, all of which contributed to establishing rapport and convincing their victims of their sincerity. By employing manipulation to build trust, both criminals exerted control over their victims, allowing them to carry out their despicable acts undetected. This manipulation also intensified the psychological trauma experienced by the victims, as they were coerced into compliance and subjected to unimaginable horrors. Powers's and Landru's criminal activities were significantly influenced by their psychological traits and psychotic tendencies. These individuals exhibited specific characteristics that enabled them to manipulate others effectively and execute their crimes with calculated precision.

Narcissism: Both Powers and Landru demonstrated narcissistic traits, displaying an inflated sense of self-importance and a lack of empathy for their victims. Their primary focus was on fulfilling their own murderous desires, regardless of the consequences to themselves or others.

Charisma: Powers and Landru possessed charismatic personalities, allowing them to easily exert influence and manipulate others. Their charm, charisma and unassuming looks enabled them to quickly establish connections, ensuring the trust and compliance of their victims.

Psychopathy: Both killers exhibited psychopathic traits, characterized by a lack of remorse, shallow emotions and a proclivity for manipulation and deceit. Their non-empathetic, cold and calculated demeanor allowed them to carry out their crimes without emotional hesitation.

These psychological traits, coupled with their manipulative tactics, contributed to the success and longevity of their criminal activities, leaving a trail of devastation in their wake. Powers, a master of manipulation and subterfuge, possessed sociopathic tendencies that he skillfully concealed behind a charming façade. By skillfully offering a sense of security, he was able to lure in his victims, ultimately leading to their unfortunate and deadly demise. In a similar fashion, Henri Désiré Landru exhibited many psychopathic characteristics. He combined his cunning intelligence with charismatic charm, employing these qualities to manipulate and deceive others. Concealed beneath a veil of sophistication, his predatory nature made him a formidable adversary. It is evident that both Powers and Landru shared a comparable psychological profile. Both individuals displayed manipulative attributes and a propensity for deception, carefully disguised under an outwardly harmless demeanor. Importantly, they exhibited traits commonly associated with serial killers—a lack of empathy and a disregard for human life, enabling them to mercilessly prey on their victims without remorse. Powers committed crimes driven by strong financial motivations. He specifically targeted vulnerable individuals, particularly single women seeking companionship and financial stability. Powers used his charm and cunning to lure his victims with promises of love, marriage and a new life together. Through this manipulation, he gained their trust and eventually ended their lives to gain access to their assets. His primary objective was to fulfill his desire for financial gain.

In contrast to Powers, Landru, also known as the "Bluebeard of Gambais," was motivated by a need for power and control over others. His criminal activities were characterized by a pattern of manipulation and dominance, targeting emotionally vulnerable women seeking connection and stability. Landru would establish relationships with his victims, gradually gaining their trust, before ultimately taking their lives and casually disposing of their remains. Through exerting power and control over his victims, Landru fulfilled his deep-seated desire for dominance and, most of all, control. Although Powers and Landru possessed distinct motives for their criminal actions, there are notable similarities between their underlying motivations. Both individuals sought personal gain through their crimes. Powers aimed for financial gain, while Landru sought a twisted sense of power and control. Both also had an insatiable lust for murder. Their respective motives stemmed from a manipulative and deceitful nature, using their victims solely as a means to an end. The manner in which they exploited the vulnerabilities of others and manipulated them for their own advantage highlights the disturbing parallel in their predatory motives.

When examining the lives of notorious serial killers, it becomes evident that their backgrounds and upbringing played a crucial role in shaping their criminal tendencies. In the next section, we delve into the peculiarities of their early lives and the events that laid the foundation for their later gruesome actions.

BACKGROUND AND UPBRINGING
OF POWERS AND LANDRU

Powers, originally known as Herman Drenth, emerged as a chilling figure from the annals of crime during the 1920s. Born in the Netherlands in 1893, Powers made his way to the United States, assuming the false identity of Harry F. Powers. Growing up under dire circumstances marked by poverty and domestic violence, Powers faced numerous challenges from an early age. These adverse experiences undoubtedly contributed to the distorted lens through which he viewed interpersonal relationships and ultimately paved the way for his descent into criminality.

Another prominent figure within the realm of serial killers, Landru operated in France during the early 1900s. Born in 1869, Landru's upbringing offers a striking contrast, seemingly stable compared to that of Powers. Raised in a working-class family, Landru cultivated an outwardly ordinary life with a wife and four children. However, beneath the surface, glimpses of his manipulative and dishonest tendencies began to manifest. Particularly in matters of finance, Landru exhibited a flair for deception, a trait that would later find expression in his sinister crimes.

ANALYSIS OF PREVIOUS CRIMINAL ACTIVITIES OF BOTH KILLERS

Before embarking on their infamous killing sprees, both Powers and Landru dabbled in the world of criminal activities. Powers, with his cunning and charm, engaged in an array of scams and fraudulent schemes to exploit unsuspecting victims. Donning various false personas and feigning different professions, he preyed on vulnerable individuals, proficiently capitalizing on their vulnerabilities. In a similar vein, Landru, a master manipulator in his own right, specifically targeted lonely widowed women, profiting from their financial resources before ultimately murdering them and disposing of their remains.

When delving into the realm of criminal activity, it becomes evident that Harry F. Powers, through his nefarious pursuits, displayed a discernible inclination toward victims who were not only vulnerable but also yearning for companionship and romantic connection. Powers specifically set his sights on single, middle-aged women who had recently endured the loss of a spouse due to the heart-wrenching circumstances of death or the distressing turmoil of divorce. These individuals, still grappling with the emotional aftermath of their personal tragedies, became easy targets for Powers's manipulative stratagems, for his alluring promises of love and an ostensibly improved life struck a deep chord within their vulnerabilities.

In striking contrast, Henri Désiré Landru adopted a different modus operandi, one centered on affluent, middle-aged women seeking both companionship and financial security. Landru specifically sought out widows who possessed considerable wealth and financial assets. By skillfully weaving webs of romantic partnership with these vulnerable individuals, Landru shrewdly exploited their deep emotional needs, successfully manipulating them for his own personal gain, much like Powers.

Examining the typologies of these victims, it becomes apparent that despite their contrasting demographics, both Powers and Landru shared a commonality in their objective: identifying and targeting emotionally fragile individuals in search of empathetic support and companionship. Both malefactors relied heavily on the vulnerability and emotional fragility that often manifested in middle-aged women, employing intricate webs of deception and deceitful tactics to establish trust and subsequently execute their sinister plans.

CONFIDENCE IN DECEIVING LAW ENFORCEMENT AGENCIES EXHIBITED BY POWERS

Powers displayed an unwavering confidence in his ability to outsmart law enforcement agencies. Despite his engagement in criminal activities, Powers firmly believed that he could continue his reign of terror without being apprehended. This confidence can be attributed to his meticulous planning, adeptness at manipulating his victims and overall cunning nature.

In a similar vein, Landru skillfully exploited the loopholes present within the legal system to evade capture. Through his mastery of deception and manipulation, Landru carefully crafted an image of an innocent individual, making it exceedingly challenging for authorities to suspect his involvement in the disappearances of his victims. He persistently maintained the belief that his actions would go undetected, ultimately leading to his successful escape from the clutches of the authorities.

COMPARISON OF BELIEFS AND ATTITUDES TOWARD EVADING CAPTURE

When comparing the two criminals, Powers and Landru, it becomes evident that both of them demonstrated an unwavering belief in their ability to elude capture. Their confidence was rooted in their successful acts of deception and manipulation, enabling them to remain undetected for prolonged periods. Additionally, both Powers and Landru shared a common ideology of exploiting the vulnerabilities inherent within the system, thereby outwitting law enforcement agencies. This shared belief underscores the striking resemblance in their attitudes toward their capacity to get away with their heinous crimes.

In examining the similarities between Harry F. Powers and Henri Désiré Landru, noteworthy parallels in both their methods and psychological profiles have been uncovered. These individuals were skilled in manipulation and deceit, employing these tactics to their advantage, thanks to their unique psychological traits. Furthermore, their motives bear striking resemblance, encompassing both financial gain and a thirst for power and control. Notably, their backgrounds also shaped them into similar types of criminals, targeting identical victims and demonstrating an uncanny confidence in eluding law enforcement agencies.

The broader significance of their respective crimes sheds light on recurring patterns in the behavior and criminal activities exhibited by notorious murderers throughout different historical eras. The results underscore the notion that individuals who possess similar personal traits and backgrounds are inclined toward similar patterns of criminal conduct, regardless of their temporal or regional context.

In terms of implications for understanding serial killers across different periods, these insights hold immense potential for the fields of forensic psychology and criminology, offering invaluable assistance to law enforcement agencies in establishing profiles and capturing such criminals more effectively. By recognizing the commonalities shared by infamous figures like Powers and Landru, we may foster an enhanced comprehension of the intricate workings of criminal minds, ultimately empowering us to refine strategies aimed at their detection and deterrence. A final noteworthy thought is that the criminal profiles of Powers and Landru are not much different from that of contemporary serial killers. In short, only time has changed—motives, however, not so much. Most, if not all, predators turned serial killers have a belief in their own impunity—that they are too clever to get caught. Yet those from the past (and many in the present) almost always get caught and tend to suffer a similar fate as that of Powers and Landru, two manipulative architects of murder.

EPILOGUE

THE ARCHITECT OF MURDER

It's no secret that an architect builds things. In the case of Harry F. Powers, he was a person who enjoyed building situations that would almost always result in murder. His toolkit consisted of mass manipulation, charm, broken promises and rope for strangulation. His victims were blinded by his charm and believed the lies that he told about owning highly profitable businesses.

Throughout the book, I use the term *vulnerable* to describe his victims. The truth is that everyone is vulnerable—everyone has a subset of vulnerabilities that can be easily exploited. The deadly thing about a personality such as Powers is how adept he was at quickly discerning the vulnerabilities of the women who placed lonely hearts ads. The *Lonely Hearts Magazine* was a predator's wonderland. Much like how Match, Plenty of Fish, OkCupid, eHarmony and a host of other online dating apps provide predators a play space to explore the endless possibilities of ensnaring a victim with ease. A recent example of the mindset of a personality like Powers in action is the Craigslist Killer. As of 2021, there were a total of 132 homicides that occurred as a result of an ad placed on Craigslist. Now, most of these homicides were not romantic in nature, but the basic premise was there— that is, someone in a vulnerable situation answers an ad placed by someone whose sole intent was to take the money from the vulnerable person, not deliver the product or service, and murder them. For Powers's victims, it was love and most importantly marriage (where marriage was a contractual arrangement or an agreement turned commodity), and for the victims of the many Craigslist Killers it was a car, gun sale, gig opportunity, sexual service or illicit service.[24]

Architects build possibilities, and an architect of murder seizes every possibility to get his victim where he wants them, which is in a situation that makes committing the murder easy. A huge part of building the murder event is in the planning phase. Serial killers like Powers enjoy the planning just as much as the execution.

> *No matter how careful their planning, for most violent and predatory criminals, since crime is essentially an irrational act in any society that prohibits it, there is often a point in which logic and reason breaks down.*
> —*John Douglas, author of* Mindhunter

The above quote is quite relevant to the criminal activities of Harry F. Powers. Was there truly ever a point where logic and reason broke down during the commission of the crimes? Absolutely. For starters, during the initial interrogation, he refused to take any accountability for the murders. He flat-out denied knowing anything about the remains of the two women and children on his property. Further, he maintained an unassuming nonchalant attitude when questioned about the erection of the garage and subterranean cells. He never maintained innocence, but he refused to admit to knowing anything about the murders. When he was beaten (it's been almost one hundred years, and it was quite evident from photographs and witnesses within the police unit that he was beaten), he began to admit to the crimes. He did this not out of guilt but out of his desire to not be hit anymore. His narcissism knew no bounds, and even after he confessed, he still played mind games. During the confession, he defaulted to playing the blame game, qualifying his former statements by acknowledging he drove to Massachusetts to pick up Dorothy Lemke but alleging she *chose* to leave him before they got to West Virginia and met up with a "friend" at a restaurant. This was his attempt to blame the victim while simultaneously portraying himself as the "true" victim. Thankfully, it did not work, and the police did not believe him. Powers told so many conflicting stories and blatant lies during questioning that the police grew as frustrated as the roaring public who stood outside of the theater. He also blamed a man by the name of Carl Rogers. Deflection was a mainstay during the confession of Harry F. Powers.

The point in which logic and reason broke down for him was when he killed young Harry Eicher. Court testimony and the coroner's report revealed that young Harry fought for his life. There was a significant amount of skin beneath his fingernails that indicated how much he fought his attacker.[25] The fighting incited rage, which is where logic and reason broke down for Powers and triggered him to grab a hammer and beat a hole in the child's head. That part of the murder was not planned, nor did it go as planned, because the whole idea here is that in Powers's mind, killing these women and children had to be easily explainable or rationalized. In that moment when he killed Harry Eicher, he could no longer justify the homicide. In that moment, Harry Eicher was no longer a vulnerable (and expendable) pawn—he became a problem that needed to be eliminated. That's a key "gotcha" moment that could never be rationalized because it indicates that even for an instant, Powers had lost control over one of his victims.

LEARNING HOW TO GET INSIDE THE MIND OF THE MURDERER WILL PREVENT READERS FROM BECOMING VICTIMS

Powers had no plans of stopping his crime spree, and there were at least three other women he was in contact with: Virginia Bell of Hagerstown, Maryland; Bessie Storries of Orleans, New York; and Edith Simpson of Detroit, Michigan, who mentioned that she was supposed to marry him within the month of September 1931.[26] These women would have undoubtedly been murdered and disposed of just as Lemke, Eicher and the children were. His plans were laid out, and had he not been caught, there would have been a trail of lonely hearts and bodies from West Virginia to Michigan. The disturbing thing here is that he never mentioned harming his wife or sister-in-law, which is an indicator that in some way, in order for his plan to work, those two women had to remain alive. As a psychopath, he viewed his victims as a means to an end. His end goal was to take all of the money from his targets, and he would stop at nothing to do so.

There are a tremendous number of people in the world today who operate like Powers. They are deadlier because they can rely on social media and modern technology to attain their goals.

You can tell by how an offender manually strangles his victim if he genuinely intends to kill, and if there are any reservations, moral hesitation or empathy.
—*John Douglas*

117

There is no doubt that Powers intended to kill each and every one of his victims, including the children. His preferred method of murder was strangulation. There are three types of strangulation: hanging, ligature strangulation and manual strangulation.[27] Each is distinguished by the amount of pressure put around the neck to cause death. Hanging results in the constriction of a band placed around the neck, and both body weight and gravitational force are contributing factors in death. Ligature strangulation occurs when a band constricts around the neck due to a force other than body weight. Manual strangulation occurs when hands or arms constrict around the neck, resulting in death. In chapters 1 and 2, I mentioned that the police found rope in the rafters of a room beneath the garage during the preliminary component of the investigation. The rope was a strong indicator of ligature strangulation. However, Powers admitted (while in prison) that he enjoyed the sensation that he felt when he strangled his victims. What is clear is that in order to strangle his victims, he preferred to be in proximity. This is the hallmark of a perpetrator who enjoys the power and control that he has when taking a life. In response to the quote above, Powers had no hesitation, nor did he have remorse for the murders that he committed.

PLANNING AND EXECUTION

In his interview with serial murderer Ed Kemper, John Douglas noted that each crime starts in the criminal's mind as a fantasy, and when it comes to fruition, there is a bit of excitement that they can now actually act out what was once a dream in their mind's eye. Manipulation, domination and control are always motivators. It is all about power and control over others. Serial killers tend to be clever and impeccably organized, their slayings well planned; they are well aware of the nature of their actions.

How they control the victims is planned out as well. Each aspect of the crime is infused with the elements of manipulation, domination and control. The serial killer will "act" or manipulate the behaviors of the victim(s) in order to ensure that the victim complies with their ultimate goal, which is murder. In the case of Kemper, he feigned being suicidal to regain control over two of his victims through manipulating their feelings to be more compliant; "he manipulated them by resolving their behaviors until they got to a place where they could be killed."[28] On controlling the situation prior to the murder of Mary Anne Pesce, Kemper mentioned that he'd spent twenty minutes arguing with her, and after he "secured" her (tied her up), she tried to gain control of the situation because she realized what the endgame was. Kemper felt that in this instant his victim managed to gain control of the situation, and he knew he had to get that control back in order to kill her. In his words, "She had already decided that I was in control, but I was trying to gain control because I was convinced that she was in control of it [the situation]." So he argued with the victim for twenty minutes over what was going to happen, and he said that he was trying to steer the argument away from what he planned to happen, which was murder. In order to regain control over the situation and the victims, Kemper changed his behavior, pretended to be suicidal and in need of help from the victims—a most sick and twisted game. His behavior reflected neediness, being suicidal, wanting help but not knowing how to ask for it, appealing to the victims' sense of empathy. He knew this would bolster a sense of sympathy for him from his victims, and he played this card until their behaviors softened and they began to trust him. Then he killed them.

This is important because it was a serial killer's admission that for a brief moment, he feared losing control to his victim. Further, it provides a visual as to what may have occurred between Harry F. Powers and young Harry Eicher. If anyone wondered how it was possible for Powers to have domination over a total of five people, the aforementioned provides a suitable explanation of how control and domination over others aids the serial killer in accomplishing the murder. If only those victims could see inside the minds of the serial killers, they would have been able to capitalize on the serial killer's loss of control. These types of predators lack the ability to empathize or be rational. At best, they feign empathy and mimic certain emotions, almost always to achieve their intended goal: murder.

NATURE VERSUS NURTURE

Nature versus nurture always comes into play with serial killers. Did something happen to them in their childhood that inspired their murderous behaviors? Was there something in their genetic makeup that inspired them to kill, such as low levels of monoamine oxidase (better known as MAOA, or the "Warrior Gene") leading to higher rates of aggression? This is always a question that comes up when reviewing the crimes of serial killers. In the case of Powers, there is limited information on his relationship with his parents.

Of particular importance is the relationship that he had (if any) with his mother. Usually, when there is a serial killer targeting women, he or she more than likely had a strained relationship with their mothers. The fact that Powers took advantage of and then murdered women could indicate that he had an issue with his own mother. His family farmed, but that was not the life for him. Somewhere in his youth or adolescence, there was a hairpin trigger that indicated an issue with his mother. Did she reject him in some way? If so, then it would make sense that rejection from the mother would result in Powers committing crimes in which women had to pay financially and with their lives. Further, could there have been a lack of an opportunity to bond with his mother or father? Sometimes it is the lack of bonding that leads to a lack of understanding or experiencing trust, which can also lead to an absence of empathy. All of these things are tied together.

> *A manipulator is not created overnight.... There is a track record.*
> —*John Douglas*

Powers was also a pathological liar. He lied to the victims; he lied to the police. He may have even believed his own lies. He did not readily offer up the truth, instead preferring to deflect until he was forced to answer questions truthfully, which brings me to the fact that it is possible that there were additional victims whose remains were never found. Powers kept letters from the various women he intended to fleece, and it could be possible that he kept some sort of documentation (hidden) recording the names of any other victims. His crimes were a complete reflection of who he was as an individual. His victims were always victims of opportunity; however, he did not sexually assault any of them. Powers mentioned that the feeling he got from watching his victims die "beat any cathouse that I [he] was ever in." Therefore, he enjoyed the power that he had over his victims—he enjoyed the control that he had over their lives. He literally admitted to achieving a heightened sexual arousal as he strangled his victims, watching their bodies struggle for air as the life left their eyes.

All serial killers like to relive the moments that they murdered their victims. Many keep mementos or souvenirs. For Powers, the souvenirs were in the form of the clothes of his victims. In his review of the case, author Douglas MacGowan mentioned that Powers's wife, Luella Strother, told police that "she never asked him about anything...[and] enjoyed the stylish women's clothing he occasionally brought her, but it never crossed her mind to ask where they had come from."[29] More than likely these "stylish clothes" belonged to Eicher, Lemke or victims who may not have been found. Serial killer Robert Hansen, better known as the "Butcher Baker" of Alaska, also gave his wife gifts or mementos that once belonged to his victims. Hansen's wife was also none the wiser to the crimes that her husband committed, nor did she realize that the gifts he gave her belonged to women he murdered. The pathology of these types of serial killers is almost always on the dark triad.

The motivation of killers like Powers is not only the money but also the hunt. They enjoy the hunt. For Robert Hansen, he stalked and hunted his victims in a manner similar to the way that he hunted animals. For Powers, the hunt occurred through the lonely hearts ads, and then he zeroed in on the perfect victim through his letters. Each letter helped him flesh out his list of potential victims, always searching for that one particular victim who could bring his fantasy to life. Powers, like all perpetrators, thought about these moments and planned every detail of each murder so that it would correspond with the murder fantasy in his mind. Many true crime aficionados may think that he committed the murders in haste, but this is wrong. Powers planned to murder each victim he lured into his web of deceit from the lonely hearts ads. Everything was always meticulously planned in his head. He carried them with him daily. He repressed them—these fantasies—held them close even, as they were his special secret, and gratification would only come when he finally had the opportunity to act them out with his victims. The murder planning is an art to predators like Powers. Its execution is like the opening night of a Broadway play. To those of us who are not psychopaths, the mere thought of it is despicable. To people like Powers, it is an art form that must be executed ever so meticulously. Put in the context of the murders of Asta Eicher and her children, he knew he was going to murder them as soon as she began corresponding with him. But much like Ed Kemper, Powers maintained control over the situation, manipulating Asta into behaving the way he needed her to behave, convincing her to agree to isolate herself from family and friends and entrust her children to him. At no time did Powers lose control or domination of the situation with Asta. He only lost control when young Harry Eicher put up a fight.

Powers had a bit of a sadistic nature in that he kept the victims in the cells in the subterranean garage prior to murdering them. The Eicher family was starved, as there was nothing in their stomachs according to the coroner's report. When they were found, they were partially bound. Again, this is an indicator of the need for the killer to maintain control and domination.

Widow and Children Here Found Murdered. *West Virginia Archives.*

MODUS OPERANDI VERSUS SIGNATURE

The modus operandi or "MO" is a learned behavior that can be shaped. The predator continually refines their MO with each criminal experience, and they gain confidence after successfully completing the criminal experience. The signature is something the predator must have in order to commit the crime—it is a personal ritual or unbreakable habit. Powers's MO had to be something that would get the captive victims to trust him. Aside from the ads placed and the coy letters, when he placed the Eichers in the murder garage, something had to have been said to somehow put them slightly at ease. He had already been around the children several times, so trust had been established. There had to be a way that they believed that he would not hurt them if they did as he asked. Maybe he was smooth and convinced the children that it was a game. Something in this vein would need to have been done in order to prevent screaming or loud cries that might draw the attention of the townspeople nearby. The same would have happened with Lemke. She had to trust that accompanying Powers into the garage was harmless. The ligature strangulation with the rope was his signature. He did not have the victims hanging in the rafters of the subterranean room in the garage, but he kept the rope there as his weapon of choice when it came to murdering the victims. Blood was found on clothes and jewelry, so unless the blood belonged to young Harry Eicher, it is possible that one of the other victims realized what Powers planned on doing and decided to fight back as well.

One contemporary serial killer that has a commonality similar to Powers is Dennis Rader, the "bind torture kill" or "BTK" killer. In his confession, he revealed that the motivation was all about the rope that he used as a ligature to kill the victims. The rope gave him additional power and dominion over the victim. It allowed him to decide the exact time when the victims would perish. It also allowed him to be the ultimate executioner, therefore satisfying the hunger and thirst for killing that lingered in the forefront of his mind. BTK was a sadist, a fetishist with a penchant for voyeurism and autoerotic asphyxiation and an avid perpetrator of zoosadism in his youth. Also, he secretly achieved sexual pleasure by dressing *en femme*; he would go as far as to put on a mask and frame it with hair prior to adding makeup to the mask. His criminal reign was from 1974 to 1991, which began exactly forty-three years after the capture of Powers in 1931. Powers also enjoyed strangling his victims using a rope, and he allegedly had his victims bound in cells beneath his garage. Both killers were married; however, BTK had children and Powers did not.

One of the key things that keeps coming up with Powers is that while his core motive was financial gain, there was never any evidence of sexual abuse or assault of the victims. This is a bit odd, but it is also an indicator of a sexual inadequacy. As mentioned earlier, Powers achieved sexual pleasure through tightening the rope during the commission of the murders and watching his victims perish. He admitted that seeing such was better than going to any brothel, which indicated that he experienced a sexual euphoria whenever he killed a victim. So his only form of sexual release came not from rape or assault but through the murder. His gratification came from inflicting pain on his chosen victims. His sexual climax came from him seeing, feeling and taking the lives of his victims.

John Robinson, a serial killer who oddly resembled Powers, was crowned the first serial killer of the internet. He managed to kill eight women, all of whom Robinson found online. He too preyed on vulnerable women, in this sense, women who unknowingly showcased their weaknesses via the need for companionship or romance online. Much like the lonely hearts ads of yesteryear, the internet is a proverbial land of unlimited opportunity for predators and serial killers alike. Robinson, like Powers, used charm to gain the trust of his intended victims.

AFTERWORD

Predators like Powers have always seemed to exist. They have always been the unknown, and elusive, hunters watching and stalking their prey in the same way that a lion or tiger might stalk its prey. These predators possess a cunning and instinctual nature, relying on their keen senses to identify vulnerabilities and strike at the opportune moment. Just like a lion silently creeping through tall grass, Powers moved unnoticed, every move calculated and deliberate. Their ability to blend into the shadows makes it difficult for their victims to detect the danger that lurks nearby. In this perpetual game of survival, these predators continue to adapt and evolve, ensuring their success as skilled hunters throughout the ages. Their cunning tactics and unparalleled stealth enable them to outsmart and outmaneuver their prey, leaving little chance for escape. Powers possessed an uncanny ability to assess his surroundings, anticipating his target's every move with precision. With each successful hunt, he and others like him solidify their position as apex predators, for they have mastered the art of silent pursuit and deadly precision. Their years of experience and honed instincts have transformed them into masters of their craft, capable of seamlessly blending into their surroundings and becoming one with society.

Being aware of these traits can help individuals be vigilant and take necessary precautions to ensure their safety. By understanding the craft of a serial killer, individuals can better comprehend the threat they pose and the tactics they employ. This knowledge can potentially save lives and aid in the identification and capture of these dangerous criminals. It also underscores the importance of community awareness and support, as the more we collectively remain vigilant, the greater our chances of preventing future tragedies. Additionally, it is crucial for law enforcement agencies to stay updated on the latest methods and strategies employed by serial killers to effectively combat this menace. Collaboration between local, state and federal authorities is essential in creating a comprehensive database of criminal profiles and patterns, aiding in the identification and apprehension of these individuals. Furthermore, enhancing public education and awareness programs can empower individuals to promptly report suspicious activities and behavior, thus strengthening the collective defense against serial killers. Ultimately, by prioritizing safety and fostering a culture of vigilance, we can work toward a society where everyone feels secure and protected from the horrors these criminals inflict.

In the shadowy alleys of our urban landscapes and the quiet corners of our suburban communities, the chilling tales of serial killers have served as harrowing reminders of the unpredictability of human behavior. Countless works have delved deep into the minds and motives of these perpetrators, revealing the intricate webs of deceit, compulsion and darkness that drive their heinous acts. Their stories serve not just as gripping tales of crime and investigation but also as cautionary tales of the dangerous underbelly that can exist in even the most seemingly idyllic settings. It underscores the importance of vigilance, community and the relentless pursuit of justice in the face of unspeakable evil. These chilling accounts expose the unsettling truth that evil knows no boundaries, infiltrating every corner of society. They remind us that behind the façade of normalcy, there may be individuals capable of unspeakable brutality. Nevertheless, they also inspire us to remain steadfast in our commitment to safeguarding our communities, encouraging us to foster stronger bonds and support networks. Ultimately, they serve as a call to action for us to never let our guard down and to continue striving toward creating a safer world for all. It is through these horrifying acts that we realize the importance of vigilance and the need to constantly address the root causes of such heinous behavior. Understanding the mindset and motives of serial killers is not just a matter of morbid curiosity or the fodder for late-night crime documentaries; it stands as an essential pillar in the fight against these deeply disturbed perpetrators. By delving deep into their psyches, we unlock more than just the grim tales of their malevolence; we open doors to invaluable insights that aid prevention and safety. Unraveling the intricate patterns, triggers and behaviors that define these predators aids law enforcement in developing more nuanced profiling tools. These detailed profiles then facilitate quicker identification and apprehension, potentially stopping killers in their tracks before they claim more victims. Furthermore, understanding their motives can lead to early intervention strategies, where individuals showing warning signs can be provided with help, hopefully diverting them from a path of violence.

Public awareness campaigns, when informed by this profound understanding, become significantly more effective. A well-informed public is better equipped to recognize potential threats in their surroundings, reducing vulnerabilities. This doesn't merely mean recognizing the actual predators; it means understanding risky situations, being more alert to manipulative behaviors and knowing how best to seek help or escape dangerous situations. Moreover, as communities become more educated on these matters, a ripple effect occurs. Neighbors look out for one another, parents educate their children on safety with greater depth and schools and institutions can enact policies that genuinely reflect the intricacies of these threats. This heightened collective awareness creates a safer environment where individuals are more vigilant, better prepared and thereby far less likely to become potential victims. Through this proactive approach, grounded in education and understanding, knowledge is not only power but also a formidable shield against the lurking shadows of danger. By educating individuals about various safety measures and potential dangers, society can empower its members to actively protect themselves and others. With a deeper understanding of these threats, parents can impart practical skills and strategies to their children, enabling them to navigate potentially risky situations. Likewise, schools and institutions can implement proactive safety protocols, ensuring that their students and staff are well-prepared to respond to any potential threat, further enhancing the overall safety of the environment. By fostering a culture of awareness and preparedness, society can effectively dismantle the vulnerabilities that criminals often exploit and cultivate a collective shield against danger.

So while the dark allure of these twisted minds may captivate us in stories, books and documentaries, it's crucial to remember that our ultimate goal is a future where such minds are understood well enough to be identified and stopped before they act. Armed with knowledge, vigilance and community support, we are better prepared to defend against the macabre manifestations of the human psyche. But even as we grow more adept at recognizing the warning signs, one can't help but wonder: Are there complex layers of the criminal mind that we have yet to uncover? As our understanding deepens, so too does the mystery, leaving us to ponder what unknown factors might still be lurking in the shadows, awaiting discovery.

NOTES

Introduction

1. Chambers, "Clarksburg."
2. Douglas and Olshker, *Mindhunter*.

1. The Whispers of the Madman

3. Douglas, Burgess and Ressler, *Crime Classification Manual*.
4. Hollandsworth, *Devil's Rooming House*.
5. Keppel, and Birnes, *Signature Killers*; Levin and Fox, *Extreme Killing*.
6. Douglas, Burgess and Ressler, *Crime Classification Manual*.
7. Holmes, *Sex Crimes*.
8. Keppel and Birnes, *Signature Killers*.
9. Michaud and Aynesworth, *Only Living Witness*.
10. Levin and Fox, *Extreme Killing*.
11. Scott, *Encyclopedia of Serial Killers*.
12. Ramsland, *Inside the Minds*.
13. Wilson and Sebesta, *Serial Killer Files*.
14. Hollandsworth, *Devil's Rooming House*.

2. The Con

15. Phillips, "True Crime."
16. Smith, "Literature of the American Serial Killer."
17. Bartlett, *Love Murders of Harry F. Powers.*
18. Cohen, "Harry F. Powers."

4. The Capture

19. Summers, *Official and Confidential.*
20. *State of West Virginia v. Harry F. Powers.*
21. Bartlett, *Love Murders of Harry F. Powers.*
22. Ibid.
23. Ibid.

Epilogue

24. Craigslist Killings, Craigslist Safety.
25. Bumgardner, "Quiet Dell Murders."
26. Ibid.
27. Sauvageau, "About Strangulation and Hanging."
28. Douglas, J. (2023) Masterclass, Lesson 2 "Becoming a Mindhunter."
29. MacGowan, *Bluebeard of West Virginia.*

BIBLIOGRAPHY

Bartlett, E.A. *Love Murders of Harry F. Powers: Beware Such Bluebeards*. New York: Sheftel Press, 1930.

Blizzard, William C. 1967. "Excitement at Quiet Dell." *Sunday Gazette-Mail*, March 26, 1967. https://www.newspapers.com.

Bottigheimer, Ruth B. "Bluebeard: A Woman's Tale." *Marvels & Tales: Journal of Fairy-Tale Studies* 25, no. 1 (2011): 37–56.

Bumgardner, S. "Quiet Dell Murders: West Virginia's Crime of the Century." *Goldenseal Magazine*, 2007.

Capote, Truman. *In Cold Blood*. New York: Modern Library, 1965.

Chambers, S. Allen, Jr. "Clarksburg." SAH Archipedia. July 13, 2018. http://sah-archipedia.org.

Cohen, Phil. "Harry F. Powers: The West Virginia Bluebeard." *Bad Endings*. February 27, 2006. www.dvrbs.com.

Craigslist Killings, Craigslist Safety. https://craigslistkillings.blogspot.com/.

Douglas, J. "Becoming a Mindhunter." MasterClass. Lesson 2. 2023. https://www.masterclass.com.

Douglas, J., A. Burgess and R. Ressler. *Crime Classification Manual: A Standard System for Investigating and Classifying Violent Crimes.* New York: Jossey-Bass, 1992.

Douglas, J., and M. Olshker. *Mindhunter.* New York: Gallery Books, 1995.

Find a Grave. "Anna N. Larsen (1850–1918)." www.findagrave.com.

———. "Asta Bothilde Buick Eicher (1881–1931)." www.findagrave.com.

———. "Dorothy Ann Pressler Lemke (1882–1931)." www.findagrave.com.

———. "Luella B. Strother Powers (1886–1957)." www.findagrave.com.

———. "Photos of Asta Bothilde Buick Eicher." www.findagrave.com.

Finnegan, Ruth H. "Bluebeard in Ireland: An Up-to-date Tale with Some Lessons on the Hinge of History." In *Chasing Tales: Travel Writing, Journalism, and the History of British Ideas about Afghanistan*, edited by Martin Green, 166–199. Leiden: Brill, 2019.

Grann, David. *Killers of the Flower Moon: The Osage Murders and the Birth of the FBI.* New York: Doubleday, 2017.

Grubb, Davis. *Night of the Hunter.* New York Harper Brothers. New York, 1953.

Haymond, Henry. *History of Harrison County, West Virginia.* Acme, 1910.

Hiben, Brittany, Jessica Jenkins and Mark Lubeskie. 2011. "Harry Powers 'Harm / Herman Drenth / Cornelius Pierson / Joseph Gildow.'" Department of Psychology, Radford University, November 13, 2011. http://maamodt.asp.radford.edu.

Holmes, R.M. *Sex Crimes: Patterns and Behavior.* Thousand Oaks, CA: Sage Publications, 2002.

Illinois Digital Newspaper Collections. "Urbana Daily Courier 3 September 1931." idnc.library.illinois.edu.

Janos, A. (2021). "Richard Beasley, Philip Markoff and Others: The Many Faces of the Craigslist Killer." *True Crime Blog: Stories & News*. August 30, 2021. https://www.aetv.com.

Keppel, Robert D., and William J. Birnes. *Signature Killers*. London: Arrow Books, 2018.

Krueger, Jewis. "Harry Powers' Murder Farm." *Morbid Tourism*. www.morbidtourism.com.

Kubberness, Gwen. "Harry Powers: Born Herman Drenth Murder." *Criminal Genealogy*. October 12, 2018. https://criminalgenealogy.blogspot.com.

Le Page Renouf, E. "Bluebeard in Sicily." *Folk-Lore Journal* 2, no. 10 (1884): 320–22.

Levin, J., and J. Fox. *Extreme Killing: Understanding Serial and Mass Murder*. Thousand Oaks, CA: Sage Publications, 2018.

MacGowan, D. *The Bluebeard of West Virginia: The Infamous Quiet Dell Murders*. Charleston, WV: Quarrier Press, 2017.

Melendez, Steven. "Albert Broel, Frog Prince of New Orleans." *Antigravity*, April 8, 2021. https://antigravitymagazine.com.

Michaud, S., and H. Aynesworth. *The Only Living Witness: The True Story of Serial Sex Killer Ted Bundy*. Authorlink, 2000.

Neikirk, Joyce. "Selvedge: The Woman's Film." *Narrative* 18, no. 3 (2010): 386–400.

Perrault, Charles. "Bluebeard." In *Mother Goose Tales*, edited by Andrew Lang, 31–36. London: Longmans, Green and Co., 1892.

Phelps, M. William. *The Devil's Rooming House: The True Story of America's Deadliest Female Serial Killer*. Guilford, CT: Lyons Press, 2010.

Phillips, Jayne Anne. "True Crime: America's Most Notorious Ladykiller." *Telegraph*, May 14, 2014. https://www.telegraph.co.uk.

Ramsland, K. *Inside the Minds of Sexual Predators.* ABC-CLIO, 2005.

Rule, Ann. *The Stranger Beside Me.* New York: Gallery Books, 2018.

Sauvageau A. "About Strangulation and Hanging: Language Matters." *Journal of Emergencies, Trauma, and Shock* 4, no. 2 (2011): 320.

Schechter, Harold. 2004. *The Serial Killer Files: The Who, What, Where, How, and Why of the World's Most Terrifying Murderers.* New York: Ballantine Books, 2004.

Scott, G. *The Encyclopedia of Serial Killers.* New York: Infobase Publishing, 2010.

Silver Salon Forums. "Shoe Buckles—SMP Silver Salon Forums." June 8, 2000. https://www.smpub.com.

Smith, Patterson. "The Literature of the American Serial Killer." *AB Bookman's Weekly*, May 9, 1988. http://www.patterson-smith.com/serialart.htm.

Smith, S. *Sons of Cain: A History of Serial Killers from the Stone Age to the Present.* New York: Berkley Books, 2016.

State of West Virginia v. Harry F. Powers. Defendant's Bill of Exceptions. Upon Indictment for a Felony No. 10357. 1931.

Summers, A. *Official and Confidential: The Secret Life of J. Edgar Hoover.* New York: Open Road Integrated Media, 2012.

Sunday Gazette-Mail. "Harry Powers Murder Story." March 26, 1967. https://www.newspapers.com.

Tabler, Dave. "Grisly Anniversary: Hanging the Bluebeard of Quiet Dell." Appalachian History. March 18, 2014. https://www.appalachianhistory.net.

Tatar, Maria. "Secrets beyond the Door: Bluebeard, Performed and Transformed." *Marvels & Tales: Journal of Fairy-Tale Studies* 17, no. 2 (2003): 269–87.

Tinnell, R., and B. Wilkerson. *Romeo Must Hang*. Morgantown, WV: Allegheny Image Factory, 2010.

Wambaugh, Joseph. *The Onion Field*. Delta, 2008.

Warner, Elizabeth Bovill. "The Twelve Brothers; Bluebeard; The Goose Girl." In *Folk and Fairy Tales: A Book of Folk and Fairy Tales from Many Lands*, edited by Katherine T. Black and Mabel Powers, 172–78. Grapevine, TX: Grapevines Press, 2016.

Warner, Marina. *Once Upon a Time: A Short History of Fairy Tale*. Oxford: Oxford University Press, 2014.

Wayback Machine. "The Bluebeard of Quiet Dell: Harry Powers, Clarksburg Serial Killer." web.archive.org.

Wenzl, Roy, Tim Potter, L. Kelly and Hurst Laviana. *Bind, Torture, Kill: The Inside Story of BTK, the Serial Killer Next Door*. New York: Harper, 2008.

Wilson, C., and J. Sebesta. *The Serial Killer Files: The Who, What, Where, How, and Why of the World's Most Terrifying Murderers*. New York: Penguin, 2007.

"WOMEN: We Make Thousands Happy." *Time* magazine, September 14, 1931.

WV Archives (1931–1932) Harry F. Powers Case File.

Zipes, Jack. "Breaking the Disney Spell." In *The Complete Fairy Tales of the Brothers Grimm*, translated by Jack Zipes, vii–xx. New York: Bantam Books, 2003.

———. *Fairy Tales and the Art of Subversion: The Classical Genre for Children and the Process of Civilization*. 2nd ed. New York: Routledge, 2006

INDEX

ABOUT THE AUTHOR

From gritty tales to groundbreaking research, Angela Fielder isn't your typical novelist. A true crime aficionado, her insights rocked the American Academy of Forensic Sciences 73rd Annual Conference and University of New Haven's electrifying Violence and Terror course—not once, but twice! When she's not crafting multilayered characters and spine-tingling plots, she's empowering law enforcement with innovative autism training. Dive into her masterful mind. With a master's degree in forensic psychology and a bachelor's in sociology, she crafts stories that stick. Dive deeper into her tales: amazon.com/author/coolgrit.

Visit us at
www.historypress.com